ENJOY
THE
BOOK

signature

Sale, Pepe, Amore & Fantasia

Salt, Pepper, Love & Creativity

Always dreamed...always wanted...here is the book.

By Marcello Russodivito

Enjoy this book.
Buon Appetito!

PUBLISHED BY

Mario Marcello Russodivito

©2005 Mario Marcello Russodivito

ISBN # 0-9767884-0-3

Printed in the Korea

First Edition

Cover design collaboration by Garry Gleason and Millicent Iacono
Cover vineyard photo by Anna Pakula
Food photography complements of Garry Gleason
Layout and book design by Millicent Iacono
Vineyard photos on pages 7 and 118-169 (except those noted otherwise) ©2005 Anna Pakula
Other photos from Marcello's family archives
Photos on page 8 by Marv Alpert – www.creativeartphotos.com, alpert@mail.com

Dedication

I would like to dedicate this book to my mother, brothers and sister in Italy, who always encouraged me to be a chef.

I would also like to dedicate this book to my wife Carolyn and daughters Nicole and Danielle, for their support and understanding of the long hours involved in operating a restaurant.

I would especially like to dedicate this cookbook to my late father Nicola Russodivito, who saw the entrepreneur in me and my late father-in-law, George, who guided me through this endeavor.

(left) Marcello's father, Nicola (center) his parents together, (right) Marcello's mother, Vittoria with baby Marcello

(left to right) Marcello's daughter Nicole, brother-in-law, Michael with his wife, Monica, father-in-law, George, daughter, Danielle, Marcello, mother-in-law, Bess and Marcello's wife, Carolyn

Introduction

Plaque donated to Marcello by the Italian government.

Since I was a child, I always tried to strive to do more, from building a fort to fundraising for my school's soccer team, to working full-time at the age of sixteen throughout Europe and then Bermuda. I think it was this full-range of life experiences that has allowed me to understand the multi-tasking profession which encompasses working while managing a restaurant.

In writing this cookbook, I wanted to not just present my recipes, but create a full and well-rounded experience of the Italian way of living. You will note that, for each recipe, I have outlined wines to compliment each dish as well as an explanation of the type of grapes and the regions you would find this wine. Not only is this a cookbook, but also a guide of suggestions and links to websites (see page 10). You can copy these links to your desktop so any time you need to learn more about Italy whether you are looking for certain products like wine, cheese, meats, or maybe you would like to inquire on a villa in Tuscany or to view the latest in Italian fashion, top restaurants or how to match food and wine, these sites are most informative.

Italian Republic president, Luigi Scalfaro and Ciao Italia president Bartolo Ciccardini honoring Marcello as Ambassador of Italian Cuisine Abroad

In June 1997, I was presented with the *Ambassador of Food and Italian Culture Abroad Award* which was presented to me by the then president of Italy, *President Luigi Scalfaro.* This award was presented to me as well as my fellow Italian entrepreneurs who live abroad and continue to make the Italian experience great. For this reason, I present to you this cookbook so that I may share my knowledge and enthusiasm with you.

Thank you and enjoy!

BUON APPETITO!

Marcello

Acknowledgements

The Italian Trade Commission for some of the information about the wine, WineAnswer.com for some tips. Also, Winebow, Tricana Imports, Lauber Imports, Kobrand Corporation, Service Liquor, Vignaioli Imports, Mionetto wines, Opici Wine, Allied Wine Company, Federal Wine Company, Colony Wine Company, Wine Emporium, Palm Bay Imports, A.V. Imports, Inc, Wine Wave Imports and Paterno Imports for providing wine label and photos.

Marco Bacci from Castello Di Bossi in Italy for providing me with some of the photographs of the vineyards in Tuscany, the staff of Marcello's of Suffern and the Ho-Ho-Kus Inn for their support, Sean J. Palmer and Michael Nelson for some of the restaurants photographs, Transformation By Design for providing props for the food photography, Allison Rose, Pat Zuzolo, Lloyd Leon, Nicole Russodivito, Carolyn Russodivito, Daniel Lagarde, Donald Avigne, Bruce Nubile, Jesse Epstein, Ramon Conception, Aniello Vacchiano for helping with corrections and food testing. Also, Erwin Elkins for helping with more corrections and the biography.

Ceramiche D'Arte from Ravello for there ceramics, Scan Pan USA, Yankee Linen for the linen, Accademia Barilla Usa, De Cecco pasta, Madison Seafood and Octopus Garden for the seafood, San Pellegrino Water, Di Marco Imports, Olio Beato Organic extra virgin olive oil, Castello Di Bossi for his olive oil, Giacomo Quagliata for Federico non-filter extra virgin olive oil, Highland & Robinson meat company and Dairyland USA and Quattro Passi Ristorante, Nerano, Sorrento, Italy and Agata e Romeo Ristorante, Rome, Italy and my brother Antonio Russodivito for final corrections.

I met Anna Pakula at a wine seminar in New York City and fell in love with her Art of Wine photographs so I decided that her photographs would be a great complement to my wine section. Below you will find a biography of my now friend, Anna Pakula.

— Marcello Russodivito

The Art of Wine

"My desire is to present wine as an integral part of life." —Anna Pakula

At early age my father instilled in me his passion for photography and my mother taught me to recognize and respect simple beauty around me. I have traveled extensively around the world and lived a multi-cultural and multi dimensional life. Born in Poland, I speak English, Polish, German, Russian, and am currently learning Italian and Spanish as well as refreshing my French.

I have diverse experience in the hospitality and wine industries of Europe, South America, and North America. I have worked and studied with winemakers and enologists throughout the world.

While living life to the fullest, I am pursuing my Pilot's license and enjoy sports. I am artistic in nature and work closely with graphic and fashion design. I love sampling the cuisine and cultures of the world. My life's goal is to "always grow" personally, professionally, and spiritually.

My photographic library contains thousands of images of the most precious and magical time in the life of fine wine. These images are derived through my passion of earth, nature and spirit. My photographic essay embodies the essence of winemaking cultivation. My photography is a vivid experience as it captures the faces and expressions of those who's hands planted, tend, nurture and work with grapevines. More specifically, it defines the moment in the grapes' life...the "miraculous harvest."

My philosophy is shared by the words of Mr. Robert Mondavi; *"Wine to me is passion, it's family and friend's warmth of heart and generosity of spirit".* "My livelihood and love for wine have taken me to striking landscapes and locations around the globe. I want to share the incredible magic of the visited grapevine territories through my photography as I have captured them through the lens."

—Anna Pakula
Photographer-Photojournalist-Wine promotion

If you wish to contact me please visit my website at:
www.homepage.mac.com/annapakula
e-mail: apakula28@aol.com

(top row) grapevines, (center) bridge in Verona Italy, (bottom row) wineries

Table of Contents

TRAVEL: When planning a trip to Italy, here are two websites that offer valuable information about Italy such as money, food, driving licenses, credit cards, accommodations, government regulations and more. www.italiantourism.com/ or www.hottraveltips.com/country/italy/index.shtml

TRANSLATING ENGLISH TO ITALIAN: Over 70 topics from accommodations to work. Each phrase is accompanied by a simple pronunciation guide which ensures that there's no problem pronouncing the foreign words. English words are in black text; Italian words are in red. Practical hints and useful vocabulary are highlighted. Where the English words appear first, this indicates vocabulary you may need. Where the red Italian words appear first, these are words you are more likely to see written on signs and notices. You will find this website very interesting: http://www.tiscali.co.uk/reference/phrases/italian/

RENTING A VILLA in Italy, visit these websites: **To request a catalog of villas visit us online at www.parkervillas.com or call us at (800) 280-2811** www.villaluciano.com www.castellodibossi.it/en/agriturismo.htm

IF you are on the Amalfi Coast and you would like to rent a boat please visit my website www.marcellosgroup.com and visit my shopping store.

SICILY is on the heart of many people. Visit this website to know more about Sicily. www.bestofsicily.com

FOOD AND WINE products, region by region including great recipes, food library and more. www.italianmade.com

TO CREATE AN INSTANT LINK: You can copy and paste the link into your browser or copy and paste link onto a blank Microsoft Word document, hit return and click on the link now underlined. This will take you to the web page.

COOKING CLASSES in Rockland County, N.Y. visit my website for more information at www.marcellosgroup.com or www.whoscookingusa.com In N.Y. City: www.italiancookingandliving.com or www.rusticocooking.com.

• Marcello is now taking reservations for 2006 tours and cooking classes in Italy together with local chefs. In Tuscany at Villa Luciano: www.villaluciano.com In Sorrento/Amalfi Coast at Ristorante Quattro Passi: www.ristorantequattropassi.it. For more information, email Marcello at info@marcellosgroup.com

• If you would like to take a cooking class near Lake Garda being held at the famous Winery Allegrini visit: www.giulianohazan.com/school/

• For professional cooking classes, Accademia Barilla has opened a professional cooking school in Parma, Italy: www.academiabarilla.com/index.htm

• If you have questions about recipes or wines from all over the world, visit these websites: www.wineanswers.com; www.epicurious.com or www.foodtv.com

RESTAURANTS in Italy & Europe. This site will bring you all the best restaurants with chef owners all under 40 years old: www.jre.net *For other restaurants in Italy go to:* marcellosgroup.com/Recommendations/index.html

RESTAURANTS in New Jersey visit: www.njdiningguide.com/ www.restaurantardore.com/

RESTAURANTS in New York City visit: www.newyorkmetro.com/restaurants/ www.menupages.com/

RESTAURANTS or things to do in the USA or Europe visit: www.timeout.com

FASHION is very big in Italy! Check these sites to discover the best in fashion design. www.modaitalia.net; www.ciao-italy.com

Appetizers

Melanzane Capriccio

Filled Eggplant with Prosciutto and Mozzarella Marinated in Creamy Pesto Basil Sauce

Serves 4

4 slices of eggplant
  (very thin)
2 eggs
4 slices of prosciutto
flour
4 slices of mozzarella
extra virgin olive oil to cook

For Pesto Basil Cream Sauce:
3 cloves of garlic
1/2 cup water
3 oz. pignoli nuts
1 cup mayonnaise
3 oz. Pecorino Romano cheese
1 cup extra virgin olive oil
6 oz. basil leaves
salt and pepper to taste

1 In medium pan, heat oil. In small bowl, beat eggs until blended. Dust eggplant with flour then dip into egg. Fry in heated oil until browned on both sides. Remove from oil, drain on paper towel and set aside to cool. Once eggplant is cool, place one slice each of prosciutto and mozzarella on top of eggplant and roll together. Place in deep baking dish. Repeat with remaining eggplant, prosciutto, and mozzarella.

2 To prepare the pesto basil cream sauce: Place all ingredients, except water and mayonnaise, in food processor. Mix until paste forms. Add water and mayonnaise and mix until sauce is very creamy but loose. Pour sauce over eggplant rolls. Marinate for 12 hours. Sauce will thicken upon standing. If sauce gets too thick, gradually add small amounts of water to desired consistency. Garnish with radicchio, tomatoes, basil and pignoli nuts. Serve cold.

Wine suggestion: Insolia or one of Marcello's favorites: Solia Antichi Vinai. (see page 147)

Eggplant in Sweet & Sour

1 large eggplant
1/2 cup sugar
2 stalks of celery, diced
1/2 cup balsamic vinegar
10 green olives, diced
8 oz. can of San Marzano
   plum Italian tomatoes
1 onion, diced
1/2 cup extra virgin olive oil
1/2 cup pignoli nuts
salt to taste
flour
olive oil or canola oil
   for frying

1 Dice eggplant then toss with salt. Place mixture in a colander, weigh it down and let sit for 2 hours. Dry eggplant with a towel. Toss with flour until evenly coated. Fry in olive oil until crispy. Drain on paper towel and set aside.

2 Poach celery for 2–3 minutes and set aside. Sauté onions in olive oil. Add celery, pignoli nuts, sugar and vinegar and cook over medium heat for 5 minutes. Add tomatoes and olives and cook an additional 10 minutes. Add fried eggplant and cook for 3 more minutes. Remove from heat and allow to cool.

3 Serve cold on top of toast points or warmed as an accompaniment to meat or fish.

A tavola non si invecchia.
English translation: At the table with good friends and family you do not become old.

Fette di Tonno in Salsa Mediterranea

Sliced Tuna with Spicy Mediterranean Sauce   Serves 4

1 lb. center cut tuna
salt to taste
crushed black pepper

Mediterranean Sauce:
2 hot cherry peppers
   with seeds removed
2 sweet cherry peppers
   with seeds removed
2 oz. capers
3 oz. sun-dried tomatoes
3 oz. black olives
3 cloves garlic
1 cup extra virgin olive oil
1 tbsp. chives
1 tbsp. parsley
mesclun salad

1 Season tuna with salt and coat with crushed black pepper. Heat non-stick pan, add 1 tsp. olive oil and sear tuna for 40 seconds on each side to medium-rare. Chill tuna and slice into ¼" slices.

2 Chop the cherry and sweet peppers, capers, sun-dried tomatoes, olives and garlic very fine by hand or in food processor. Add the olive oil, chives and parsley and mix it until fully combined.

3 Arrange sliced tuna on plate with mesclun salad and drizzle with sauce.

Wine suggestion: Riesling or one of NY state's best: Brotherhood Riesling. (see page 160)

Insalata di Mare

Seafood Salad

Serves 4 to 6

12 steamer clams
6 medium shrimp
1 lb. squid
1/2 pound bay or sea scallops
24 mussels, smaller is best
1/4 cup of white wine
2 tablespoons of water
1/2 cup lemon juice
1/2 lemon, thinly sliced
1/2 cup extra virgin olive oil
3 cloves of sliced garlic
2 oz. of diced celery
2 oz. of diced carrots
2 oz. parsley

1 Leave shells on shrimp. Devein by cutting along the outside curve of the shell. Rinse under cold running water. Bring a large pot of salted water to a boil. Add the shrimp and cook for 2 to 4 minutes. Drain. Let cool. Discard the shells.

2 Clean the squid carefully, or use frozen already cleaned, and poach it for 5 minutes in boiling water with salt and lemon juice, then drain it.

3 Leave bay scallops whole; cut sea scallops into squares. Repeat same cooking procedure as the shrimp and squid 2 or 3 minutes. Drain and let cool.

4 Scrub the mussels and clams well under cold running water. Remove all traces of grit and slime. The mussels in the shell will be used in the salad. Remove the beard by tugging hard at it until it breaks free from the shell. Place in a wide-bottomed pan. Add a few tablespoons of water and about a quarter cup of white wine. Cover and cook over high heat, shaking the pan while cooking to redistribute the mussels. When the mussels open, remove from the pan and let cool.

5 To assemble the salad, combine all the seafood with a generous amount lemon juice, garlic, extra virgin olive oil, salt and pepper, diced celery and carrots. Toss gently. Cover tightly with plastic wrap and marinate for 2 hours. If refrigerated, bring to room temperature before serving. Garnish with lemon slices and chopped parsley.

Wine suggestion: Regaleali Bianco. *(see page 161)*

Caprino Tiepido con Noci, Mele e Peperoni

Warm Goat Cheese Salad with Apple, Walnut, Lemon Mustard Dressing and Roasted Peppers

Serves 4

8 oz. goat cheese cut in 4 pcs.
1 cup roasted peppers
(see page 87)
1 oz. flour
1 apple sliced
1 egg white
2 oz. toasted walnuts (see right)
1 cup Japanese panco bread or
regular plain breadcrumbs
1/4 of cup olive oil

For Dressing:
1 tbsp. dijon mustard
2 tbsp. lemon juice
6 tbsp. extra virgin olive oil
salt and pepper to taste

1 Dust goat cheese with flour. Dip in egg whites then lightly coat with bread panco. In small sauté pan, heat oil and cook goat cheese until both sides are golden brown. Remove and place in oven for 6 minutes at 400°F.

2 For Salad: Use any salad greens that you like. Mix with walnuts, sliced apple and roasted peppers. For Dressing: combine all ingredients until thoroughly mixed and creamy. Mix dressing into salad greens tossing gently. Finish with warm goat cheese on top.

3 For Toasted Walnuts: Toast walnuts in a 350° oven for 5 to 10 minutes. Let the walnuts cool and add them to your favorite recipe.

Wine suggestion: Pinot Noir or one of
Marcello's favorites: Pinot Noir Brotherhood (see page 151)

Funghi Ripieni

Stuffed Mushroom Caps

16 whole mushrooms
2 oz. Parmigiano Reggiano cheese
8 oz. Italian fennel sausage
2 oz. ricotta cheese
1/2 cup extra virgin olive oil
1 cup of water or chicken stock
  (see page 28)
2 oz. sweet butter
1 oz. Italian parsley
pepper to taste

Wine suggestion: Super Tuscan or one of Marcello's favorites: Querciavalle Armonia (see page 130)

1 Separate caps from mushrooms and set aside. Chop stems. Stir-fry chopped stems and sausage in olive oil until crispy.

2 Drain excess oil. Place sausage and mushroom mixture in food processor. Add ricotta, parmigiano and some parsley. Blend together. Allow mixture to cool then spoon into mushroom caps. If desired, dot with butter.

3 Place stuffed caps in baking dish. Add water or chicken stock to just cover the bottom of dish. Bake uncovered for 15 minutes in a 400° oven.

4 Note: To make additional sauce, add ¼ cup butter and ¼ cup chicken stock to pan during the last 5 minutes of baking.

Calamari in Guazzetto con Piselli

Calamari Stew with Peas

Serves 2

1 lb. calamari
1/4 cup white wine
1/2 onion, chopped
1 cup tomato sauce
  (see page 94)
1/2 cup extra virgin olive oil
red pepper to taste
1 cup frozen peas
salt and pepper to taste

1 In a medium pan, sauté onions with olive oil for 1 minute. Add calamari and peas, stir fry for an additional 3 minutes. Add wine. Once wine has evaporated, season with salt and pepper. Add red pepper and tomato sauce and cook for 2-3 minutes. Serve with Italian garlic bread (see recipe page 90)

2 Note: If using fresh calamari, ask for baby calamari, cleaned and sliced very thin. If using frozen calamari, make sure it is a good quality. Frozen calamari may take longer to cook.

Wine suggestion: Fiano D'Avellino or one of
Marcello's favorites: Fiano D'Avellino Terredora (see page 146)

Gratinata di Vongole al Pane Agliato

Clams Oreganata

Serves 4

24 clams (little necks)
3 garlic cloves, chopped very fine
2 oz. chopped parsley
1 cup plain breadcrumbs
1/2 cup extra virgin olive oil
1 tbsp. dry oregano
black pepper to taste
no salt
4 lemon wedges

1 Open clams and save some of the juice. Put clams in a baking pan. In a small bowl combine breadcrumbs, garlic, olive oil and herbs. Mix together well and put a little bit of breadcrumbs on top of each clam. Bake the clams at 400° for 15 minutes. Serve with wedges of lemon.

2 If you would like to have a butter sauce with the clams, combine 2 oz. of butter and the clam juice that you saved and 1/4 cup of dry white wine. Add the liquid to the clams at the last 5 minutes of baking and serve with lemon wedges.

Wine suggestion: Greco di Tufo or one of
Marcello's favorites: Greco di Tufo Mastroberardino (see page 146)

Polpette di Granchio

Crabcakes with Remoulade

Makes 8 Crabcakes

1 lb. lump crabmeat
2 cups Japanese panco breadcrumbs
1 lemon rind, chopped fine
1/2 cup flat leaf parsley, chopped
3 tbsp. dijon mustard
1/2 cup red onion, chopped fine
3 tbsp. mayonnaise
1/4 cup chopped chives
1 tbsp. worcestershire sauce

Remoulade:
1 cup sour cream or mayonnaise
3 apples, shredded
2 oz. horseradish
1 teaspoon black pepper

1 To Assemble Crabcakes: Mix together all ingredients with only a ¹/₂ cup of breadcrumbs. Form into cakes about 2" in diameter and about ¹/₄" high. Coat with breadcrumbs. Heat olive oil in a non-stick fry pan. Add crabcakes and sauté for 1¹/₂ minutes on each side over medium heat. Remove from pan and bake an additional 5 minutes in a 400° oven.

2 For Remoulade: Shred apple and place in a clean, dry cloth. Squeeze to remove juice. Combine apple and remaining ingredients and mix thoroughly.

3 To serve, place crabcakes on a plate with about a teaspoon of remoulade on the side. Garnish with greens of your choice.

Wine suggestion: Seyval or one of Marcello's favorites: Brotherhood Seyval Blanc (see page 161)

Lumachine in Guazzetto di Funghi e Pomodoro

Snails Sautéed with Mushrooms & Garlic in White Wine and Tomato Sauce
Serves 4

3 oz. butter
4 cloves garlic, crushed
2 cups tomato sauce
  (see page 94)
1/4 cup dry white wine
1/2 cup chicken or vegetable
  stock (see page 28)
1 oz. chopped parsley
32 pieces of canned or frozen
  snails (good quality)
4 oz. shiitake or bottom
  mushrooms, sliced
salt and pepper to taste
Italian or French bread

1 In medium saucepan, combine butter and garlic and heat until butter is just melted. Add mushrooms and continue cooking over low heat.

2 Drain and dry snails then add to pan. Cook for 2 minutes stirring occasionally. Add wine and cook until wine has evaporated.

3 Add chicken stock and tomato sauce. Cook an additional 5 minutes over low heat. Serve with garlic bread (see page 90).

Wine suggestion: Pinot Noir or one of Marcello's favorites: Pinot Noir from Brotherhood Winery. (see page 151)

Polipetti alla Griglia con Patate, Capperi & Pomodoretti

Baby Octopus with Potato, Capers & Oven Roasted Tomato
Serves 4

4 baby octopus
2 poached potatoes with skin
  diced in small cubes
1/2 onion, chopped
2 oz. capers
3 oz. cherry tomatoes
  oven roasted, optional
1/2 cup extra virgin olive oil
1/2 oz. chopped Italian parsley
1 lemon skin
2 cloves of garlic, sliced
salt pepper to taste

Wine suggestion:
Fiano D'avellino Terre Dora (see page 146)

1 Marinate the octopus with lemon skin sliced, 1 clove garlic, a little olive oil and a pinch of salt and pepper for a few hours. Then grill the fish for 3 minutes on each side.

2 In a sauté pan, heat oil, add onion and garlic and cook for 1 minute. Add potatoes and cook for additional 2 minutes. Then add capers, pinch of salt, pepper and stir for a few more seconds. Next add oven roasted tomatoes and chopped parsley. Last add the octopus on top of the potatoes and serve it with little extra virgin olive oil.

3 *For oven roasted tomatoes:* Put tomatoes in a baking pan with a little olive oil, salt and pepper and roast at 275° for two hours.

Bresaola

Bresaola technically refers to beef that has been rubbed with spices, like rosemary and thyme, and air-cured. Bresaola originated in the Valtellina Valley in Lombardia, where Italians first began stringing pieces of beef up to cure in the cool air of that long Alpine valley. Though it is lean, much leaner than other Italian cured meats, and it's sweet smell has a definite musty note, the meat itself is succulent and tender. When thinly sliced, bresaola is beautiful to behold, an almost transparent, jewel-colored slip of tender meat. It should always be sliced paper thin, and is delicious when prepared simply, as it is most often eaten. Sliced and dressed with a drizzle of extra-virgin olive oil, a squirt of lemon juice, and a smattering of freshly cracked black pepper, bresaola may be at its best.

You can also serve bresaola topped with arugula freshly shaved Parmigiano-Reggiano, capers and drizzle of extra-virgin olive oil, a squirt of lemon juice, and a smattering of freshly cracked black.

Wine suggestion: Barbera or one of Marcello's favorites: Barbera D'Alba Baricchi. (see page 123)

Cotechino con Lenticchie

Cotechino with Lentils

8 oz. dried lentils,
   preferably black lentils
1 tbsp. salt
2 cloves garlic
12 fresh sage leaves
4 tbsp. extra-virgin olive oil
4 tbsp. red wine vinegar
salt and freshly ground
black pepper, to taste
1 lb. cotechino sausage

Wine suggestion: Chianti or
one of Marcello's favorites: Rocca
delle Macie Chianti (see page 128)

1 Bring 6 cups of water to a boil and add 1 tablespoon salt. Add the lentils, garlic and sage. Boil the lentils until they are tender yet still firm, about 20 minutes. Drain and place in a mixing bowl. Combine the lentils with the vinegar and season with salt and pepper.

2 Prick the sausage with a fork several times. Place in a large pot of cold water and bring to a boil over medium heat. Reduce the heat to a simmer(slow boiling) and cover the pot. Cook for $1\frac{1}{2}$ hours. In some stores you can find cotechino precooked then you only need to warm it up for 20 minutes.

3 Place the marinating lentils on a large serving platter. Remove the cotechino from the cooking liquid and drain. Slice the sausage into $\frac{1}{4}$-inch rounds and place over the lentils. Serve immediately.

Cotechino

Traditional to Emilia-Romagna, Cotechino with Lentils is a crucial part of the Italian New Year's Eve's meal. The lentils symbolizing money and the sausage itself signifying luck, the dish promises prosperity in the new year.

Compared to other sausages, cotechino is a bit large, usually at least 3 to 4 inches in diameter and 7 to 8 inches long. Made entirely of fresh pork taken from the cheek, neck and shoulder of the pig, the sausage is usually flavored mildly, with only nutmeg, cloves, salt and pepper.

A tavola non si invecchia.
English translation: At the table with good friends and family you do not become old.

Caprese con Mozzarella di Bufala

Caprese Salad of Mozzarella & Tomato   Serves 2

8 oz. Bufala mozzarella or
   fresh regular mozzarella, sliced
2 ripe tomatoes
4 leaves fresh basil
2 tbsp. extra virgin olive oil
1 tsp. dry oregano
salt and pepper to taste

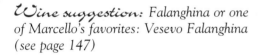

1 Place the sliced tomato on a plate. Top each piece with a slice of mozzarella and basil leaf. Drizzle each one with extra virgin olive oil season with little oregano, salt and pepper.

BUFALA MOZZARELLA

Bufala mozzarella is a snowy-white, delicate, fresh cheese with a slightly fibrous consistency resulting from the multitudinous layers from which it is comprised. Made entirely of whole Bufala milk, it is inoculated with a starter culture of the previous day's whey. After about 30 minutes the milk begins to coagulate and the cheese maker breaks the curd into small pieces to ripen for 5 hours, after which time the curd is transferred to a boiling vat for stretching. It is sold either in baseball-sized balls or in smaller balls called bocconcini.

Mozzarella di Bufala has a slightly sour tang that is offset by a creamy, milky bite. The cheese is produced almost exclusively in Campania. It is an essential part of Naples' wood-fired pizza and is often served on its own or with prosciutto or famous Mozzarella Caprese.

Wine suggestion: Falanghina or one of Marcello's favorites: Vesevo Falanghina (see page 147)

Soup

Pasta e Fagioli
White Bean Soup

Serves 4

1 lb. cannellini beans
2 tbsp. extra virgin olive oil
1 stalk of celery
1/4 cup extra virgin olive oil
1 onion, chopped
2 bay leaves
6 oz. pancetta or prosciutto
2 cloves garlic, chopped
salt and pepper to taste

Wine suggestion:
Marcello's favorites: Ramitello di Maio Norante from Molise (see page 163)

1 Soak beans overnight in cool water. Drain beans and place in saucepan. Cover with cold water and bring to a boil (about 20 minutes).

2 In separate pan, sauté celery, onions, chopped garlic and pancetta with extra virgin olive oil and black pepper. Add to beans and cook an additional 20 minutes. Season to taste.

Tip: DO NOT add salt until 3 minutes before beans are cooked. Doing so will make beans become too al dente.

3 Note: If you want to add pasta to your soup, add it 5 minutes before soup is finished cooking. Use a small variety of pasta such as vermicelli or ditalini.

Pappa al Pomodoro

Tuscan Bread Tomato Soup

1 medium onion, finely chopped
3 tbsp. olive oil
32 oz. tomatoes
4 cups chicken stock (see page 28)
1/2 cup fresh basil leaves
  (set aside some pretty leaves
  for garnish)
5-6 cups stale Italian bread cubes,
  crust removed
5 cloves garlic
salt and pepper to taste
extra virgin olive oil
1/4 cup parmigiano

1 Pass the tomatoes through a food mill. In a large pot sauté the onions in the oil until they are translucent. Add the tomatoes and broth and bring to a boil. Reduce the soup to a simmer and cook 20 minutes.

2 In a saute pan put some extra virgin olive oil with some garlic add the bread and bake until crispy. Remove garlic and add bread to the soup. Simmer for 10 more minutes. Take a whisk and break up the bread to thicken the soup. Remove from the heat.

3 To Serve: I like to serve this soup just slightly warm, garnished with a pretty sprig of basil, some cracked black pepper and a drizzle of very good olive oil and parmigiano.

This recipe is for yet another famous Tuscan soup whose name, pappa, simply means purée. It is often made in very large batches, and is always served just slightly warm or at room temperature. The addition of the bread as a thickener creates a soup hearty enough to be a main course. If you are serving this as a starter, keep the portions small. Use the best tomatoes you can find. I suggest using San Marzano tomatoes if you are using canned, or if you choose the fresh option, make sure you have very ripe, tasty tomatoes.

Wine suggestion: Sangiovese or one of Marcello's
favorites: Antinori Santa Cristina (see page 131)

Brodo di Pollo, Brodo di Pesce, Brodo di Vegetali, Brodo di Manzo

Basic Chicken, Vegetable, Beef & Fish Stock

1/2 oz. black peppercorn
1 celery stalk, diced
1 onion, diced
1 carrot, diced
1 lb. chicken bones
1 tbsp. salt
1 gallon of water

For Chicken Stock:
Poach chicken bones, vegetables and spices in cold water. Bring to full boil. Reduce heat and simmer for 1 hour. Remove from heat. Allow to cool then strain to remove chicken bones and vegetables. Store in covered container until ready to use.

For Vegetable Stock:
Follow as above except omit chicken bones.

For Beef Stock:
Follow as above except cut onion in half and roast on grill or in oven first until blackened. Substitute beef meat for the chicken bones.

For Fish Stock:
Follow as above chicken stock, substituting white fish bones such as sole, snapper or monkfish for the chicken bones. Omit carrot.

Botte buona fa buon vino.
English translation: A good cask makes good wine.

Zuppa Di Farro

Tuscan Farro Soup

1lb. Farro* (spelt)
10 cups chicken stock
  (see page 28)
1 onion, finely chopped
1/4 cup Parmigiano Reggiano
1 carrot, finely chopped
1/4 cup extra virgin olive oil
1 celery stalk, finely chopped
2 bay leaves
1 cup white wine
2 cups of San Marzano plum
  Italian tomatoes
1 tbsp. red pepper flakes
1 tbsp. black pepper
salt to taste

Wine suggestion: Montepulciano
d'Abbruzzo or one of Marcello's favorites:
Illuminati Riparosso (see page 134)

1 In a large pot, heat olive oil. When oil is hot, add onions, carrots and celery and let sweat. Add Farro and stir into vegetables until blended.

2 Mix in wine, bay leaves, garlic, red and black pepper and tomato sauce. Cook for 2-3 minutes. Add chicken stock. Bring to boil and stir every 2-3 minutes (similar to cooking Risotto).

3 When Farro absorbs almost all of the liquid (about 1 hour) the soup is ready to be served (Farro will remain al dente). Taste for seasoning.

4 To serve, pour into soup bowl, and add a couple of drops of extra virgin olive oil and some shredded Parmigiano cheese.

* Farro is a grain similar to barley and can be purchased in most specialty shops.

Wine makes daily living easier less
hurried with fewer tension and more tolerance.
—Benjamin Franklin

Crema di Carote, Mele and Zenzero

Carrot, Apple, Ginger Soup   Serves 4

5 carrots
1 onion
2 apples
4 oz. of ginger
1 large potato
6 cups of vegetable stock
   (see page 28)
1/2 cup of olive oil
1/2 cup heavy cream, optional
salt and pepper to taste

1 In a stock pot sauté the onions and carrots in olive oil for a few minutes. Add peeled apple, potatoes and ginger and cook for a few more minutes.

2 Add stock and simmer until carrots are tender. Purée the soup and add cream (optional) and taste for flavor.

Crema di Finocchi e Pomodoro

Cream of Tomato & Fennel   Serves 4

1/4 cup olive oil
1 onion, chopped
2 peeled potatoes, cubed
2 heads of fresh fennel, cubed
2 oz. San Marzano tomatoes
1 oz. fresh or dry thyme
8 leaves of fresh basil
salt and pepper to taste

1 In sauce pot, heat olive oil and saute onions. Add fennel and cook for a few more minutes, add salt, pepper and potatoes. Sweat all vegetables for 3-4 minutes and add tomatoes, thyme and basil.

2 Simmer for 35 minutes in low flame. When fennel is nice and tender put in food processor or food mill and make soup very creamy. Adjust flavor with salt and pepper and serve with Italian crustini and garnish with fresh basil.

Ribollita

Tuscan Bread, Tomato, Bean, Soup with Cabbage

1 onion, chopped
1 large zucchini diced
1 lb. savoy cabbage, chopped
2 cups dry cannellini beans or
   2 cups canned cannellini beans
2 cups plum tomatoes
2 cups vegetable stock
2 cloves garlic, sliced
10 leaves fresh chopped basil
3/4 cup tuscan extra virgin
   olive oil
1/2 lb. Italian bread, cut
   into small cubes
1/2 cup grated parmigiano
salt and pepper to taste

1 If you use dry beans soak beans over night, rinse and cover with cold water. Cook beans for 45 minutes to 1 hour. When beans are cooked season with salt and pepper.

2 In a sauté pot heat olive oil, add onions and garlic and cook for 2 minutes. Then add cabbage and zucchini and cook for 6 more minutes. Now add beans and mix together.

3 Season with salt and pepper then add tomatoes, vegetable stock and some of the basil. Cook the soup on low flame for 30 minutes. Just before serving add bread, the rest of basil and parmigiano. Cook for five more minutes and serve very hot. Add a little oil on top of each serving.

Crema di Piselli Fredda con Granchio

Cold Pea Soup with Crabmeat

Serves 4

8 oz. of lump crabmeat
1 lb. potatoes
1 onion
1 lb. frozen peas
10 cups of chicken stock or
 vegetable stock (see page 28)
1/2 cup olive oil
salt and white pepper to taste

1 Cut potatoes into small pieces. Slice onion and sauté in olive oil. Add potatoes. Cook for a few minutes, add stock and simmer it until potatoes are cooked. Then add frozen peas for 5 minutes. Put the soup in the food processor until smooth. Add salt and pepper to taste.

2 If soup is too thick, add more stock. If you want the soup very fine after the food processor, strain soup into a fine colander.

3 Serve this soup chilled. Add before serving a small amount of crabmeat.

Wine suggestion: Pinot Grigio or one of Marcello's favorites: Hofstätter Pinot Grigio (see page 140)

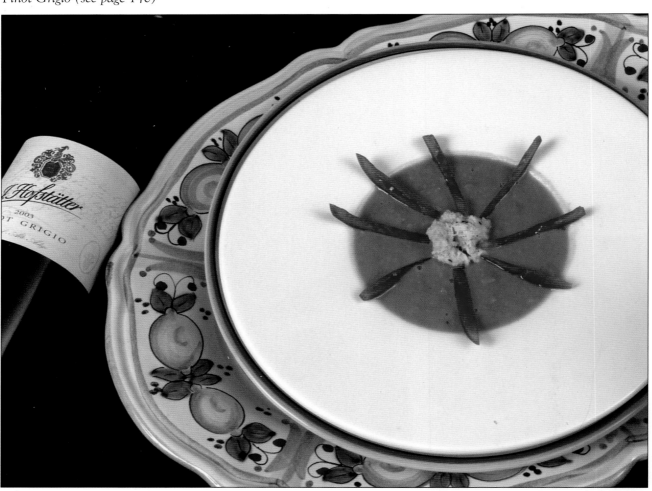

Crema di Patate & Porri

Potato & Leek Soup   Serves 8

10 potatoes
2 carrots
2 onions
5 qts. chicken stock (see page 28)
1 tbsp. shallots
1 tomato, diced very small
2 bunches of leeks,
   white part only
1/2 cup heavy cream
extra virgin olive oil
salt and pepper to taste

1 Roughly chop all vegetables and sweat them in extra virgin olive oil until onions are translucent. Add chicken stock and simmer until potatoes are thoroughly cooked.

2 Put soup through food mill, add cream and season with salt and pepper. Bring to a boil. Remove from heat and serve with tomato concase.

3 If soup is too thick, add more stock. If you want the soup very fine after the food processor, strain soup into a fine colander.

Wine suggestion: Pinot Noir (see page 151)

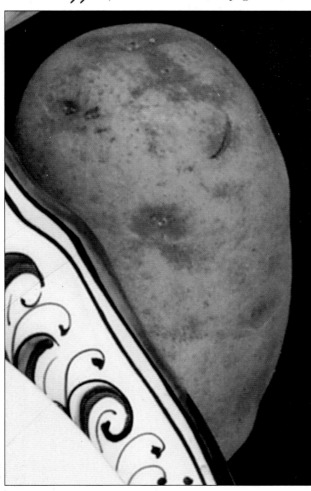
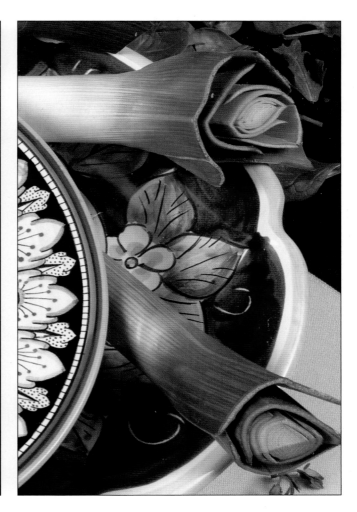

Minestrone di Vegetali

Italian Vegetables Soup

Serves 4

1 onion, chopped
2 cups diced carrots
2 cups diced celery
1 cup diced zucchini
1 cup diced potatoes
salt & pepper to taste
I cup fresh peas
1/2 cup extra virgin olive oil
1/4 cup parmigiano
2 cups water, vegetable stock
    or chicken stock (see page 28)
1 cup fresh plum tomatoes,
    chopped
1 cup parmigiano

1 Sauté onions and garlic in oil for a few minutes, then add carrots and celery and continue to cook for a least 10 more minutes.

2 Then add the potatoes and cook for 2 more minutes. Add the zucchini, peas and diced tomatoes and season with salt and pepper.

3 Add stock and simmer for 10 more minutes and the minestrone is done. Serve with garlic croutons, parmigiano cheese and a bit of extra virgin olive oil.

Pasta

Ciufoli alla Riccese

Mini Hand-made Cavatelli with Light Tomato Ragu and Sausage

Serves 4

For the no egg-fresh pasta:
1 1/2 cups of flour
  (semolina recommended)
1 cup of water
1 tbsp. extra virgin olive oil
1 tbsp. of salt

For the sauce:
12 oz. of San Marzano plum
  Italian tomatoes
4 links of Italian sausage
2 cloves of garlic
2 oz. of chopped onions
1/2 oz. basil leaves
salt, black pepper and red
  crushed pepper to taste
3 oz. extra virgin olive oil
4 oz. pecorino or parmigiano

Wine suggestion:
Montepulciano D'Abruzzo or one
of Marcello's favorites: Zaccagnini
Montepulciano D'Abruzzo (see page 134)

1 To make pasta combine flour and salt in a mixing bowl. Create a crater in the center and add half cup of water and oil. Begin to work flour toward the center while mixing in all the ingredients. As pasta begins to form, add remaining water as needed. This type of pasta needs to be a little drier than basic pasta. Knead the pasta for a few minutes, cover it and let the pasta rest for 20 minutes.

2 Roll pasta into 1/2" thick sheets trim ends and sides until the pasta roughly resembles a rectangle. Cut into 1 inch-wide strips. Cut each strip crosswise into 1/2 inch matchstick pieces. Each matchstick piece is ready to be formed into a ciufoli shape. By pressing down firmly with the tip of your finger the pasta edges will curl and form the ciufoli shape. Make sure they are very thin. Put the ciufoli with a little semolina on a wood tray or baking pan ready to be cooked.

3 For the sauce: In a sauté pan, add oil, garlic and onion. Cook for a minute, add Italian sausage. Cook slowly for five minutes, add tomato, basil, salt, pepper and crushed red pepper. Simmer sauce for 30 minutes, cook pasta al dente then toss pasta in to the sauce. Add cheese and serve it very hot. Each dish will have a sausage link.

Large-shaped Noodle with Speck, Zucchine and Parmigiano Sauce

Serves 4

1 lb. pappardelle
4 oz. speck, julienned
1 lb. baby zucchini, julienned
2 cups chicken stock (see page 28) or water from pasta
4 oz. Parmigiano Reggiano cheese, grated
2 oz. shaved parmigiano
8 oz. cherry tomatoes
2 oz. chopped chives
3 oz. butter
2 tbsp. extra virgin olive oil

1 In large pot, bring water to a boil. Add salt and pasta. Cook al dente.

2 Meanwhile, in large saucepan heat olive oil and half of butter. Add zucchini and speck. Cook about 1 minute. Add cherry tomatoes and chicken stock (or water from pasta).

3 Drain pappardelle and add to sauce. Add the remaining butter, Parmigiano and chives. Mix thoroughly. Serve in large bowl allowing the zucchini, speck and cherry tomatoes to be on top and garnish with shaved Parmigiano.

Wine suggestion: Pinot Nero or one of Marcello's favorites: Pinot Nero Torti Oltre Po Pavese (see page 151)

Maccheroni al Ragú Riccese con Polpettine a Scamorza

Pasta with Tiny Lamb Meatball Ragu and Dry Mozzarella

Serves 4

1 lb. macaroni pasta
1 lb. lamb meat, chopped
32 oz. of San Marzano plum
  Italian tomatoes
3 cloves garlic, chopped
2 oz. prosciutto
salt and pepper to taste
1/4 cup extra virgin olive oil
2 eggs
1 oz. parsley
3 pieces white bread, no crust
1/4 cup milk
8 oz. scamorza or mozzarella, cubed
3 oz. grated parmigiano or pecorino
2 oz. flour
salt and pepper to taste

Wine suggestion:
one of Marcello's favorites:
Colle Picchioni Rosso (see page 163)

1 In a bowl mix lamb, eggs, white bread soaked in milk and squeezed, salt, pepper, parsley and 1 oz. of parmigiano. You can add some garlic to meat (optional) then make very tiny meatballs.

2 Put them in a tray and dust the meat with a little flour. Fry the meatballs for a few minutes and drain on paper towels.

3 Sauté extra virgin olive oil with prosciutto and garlic. Add plum tomatoes and cook for about 20 minutes on medium heat. Add lamb meatballs and cook another 20 minutes.

4 Cook macaroni until al dente. Drain and toss with sauce and meatballs. Add small cubes of scamorza or mozzarella and parmigiano.

Makes approximately 30 tiny meatballs.

Orecchiette con Pesto di Cime di Rape e Salsiccia

Orecchiette with Broccoli Rabe Purée and Sausage
Serves 4

3 cloves garlic
1 lb. of broccoli rabe florets
1/2 cup extra virgin olive oil
3 links of Italian sausage
1/2 cup of pecorino or
  parmigiano or blend of two
1 tsp. red pepper
4 oz. cherry tomatoes (see page 21)
salt and pepper to taste

1 Poach broccoli rabe. When soft, toss it with garlic, oil, salt, pepper and a little red pepper. Blend in a food processor with parmigiano or pecorino cheese and little extra virgin olive oil.

2 Roast or boil Italian sausage for five minutes, let it cool. Cook pasta al dente. In the time pasta is cooking, cut the boiled sausage in small round pieces and sauté it with garlic and oil. Add pasta, broccoli purée and little cheese. Toss it and serve.

3 Optional: You can add some tomato sauce and some oven roasted tomatoes (see page 21) to add color to the dish.

Wine suggestion: Salice Salentino Taurino (see page 135)

Penne with Pink Vodka Sauce and Radicchio

Serves 4

4 tbsp. extra virgin olive oil
2 small shallots, chopped
2 oz. Parmigiano Reggiano or
  Grana Padano
1/4 stick of butter
4 oz. heavy cream
1 lb. penne pasta
1 lb. radicchio, julienne
1 oz. vodka
2 cups tomato sauce (see page 94)
pinch of Italian red pepper
pinch of fresh parsley

1 In medium pan, sauté shallots and radicchio in butter and olive oil. Stir for 2-3 minutes. Add red pepper and vodka and flame it.

2 Gradually add tomato sauce and heavy cream. Cook for 10 minutes over low flame. Cook pasta and cook until al dente. Drain and stir in sauce. Garnish with Parmigiano and parsley.

Wine suggestion: Valpolicella/Amarone or one of Marcello's favorites: Allegrini Palazzo della Torre (see page 125)

Riempi il bicchiere quando é vuoto, vuota il bicchiere quando é pieno,
non lo lasciar mai vuoto, non lo lasciar mai pieno.
English translation: Fill your glass when it is empty, empty it when
it is full, never leave it empty, never leave it full.

Maccheroni al Filetto di Pomodoro e Parmigiano

Pasta with Tomato and Parmigiano

Serves 4

32 oz. of San Marzano
   plum Italian tomatoes
3 cloves garlic, crushed
4 whole basil leaves
1 tsp. salt
1 tbsp. oregano
1/8 cup olive oil
12 tbsp. parmigiano cheese
1 lb. of pasta
salt to taste

1 Sweat garlic in olive oil. Add tomatoes and seasonings. Let simmer for approximately 20 minutes. Cook your favorite pasta al dente, toss it with the sauce, add parmigiano cheese.

Wine suggestion: Chianti or one of Marcello's favorites: Coli Chianti Riserva (see page 127)

Pasta al Ragu di Funghi

Pasta with Wild Mushroom Sauce

Serves 4

1/2 onion, diced
2 oz. Italian prosciutto
3 oz. butter
2 oz. extra virgin olive oil
1/2 lb. mushrooms, mixed
3 oz. Parmigiano Reggiano
3 cups tomato sauce (see page 94)
1/2 cup heavy cream
any pasta of your choice
salt and pepper to taste

Wine suggestion: Light Super Tuscan or one of Marcello's favorites: Carpineto Dogajolo (see page 130)

1 In large pot, cook pasta according to package directions. In medium pan, sauté onions with butter and olive oil. Add prosciutto and cook over medium heat for 1 minute. Add mushrooms and stir for 2-3 minutes. Add tomato sauce and heavy cream.

2 Mix thoroughly and heat until warmed. Drain pasta and toss with sauce until coated. Garnish with parmigiano.

Rigatoni all' Amatriciana

Rigatoni with Pancetta, Tomato and Pecorino

Serves 4

1 lb. of rigatoni
32 oz. of San Marzano plum
   Italian tomatoes
4 oz. pancetta
   (see glossary page188)
1/2 onion, chopped
3 oz. pecorino cheese, grated
salt to taste
red chili peppers

1 This recipe requires the rigatoni pasta shape, whose typical consistency should not be spoiled by overcooking.

2 Chop the bacon into thin bits, and cook them in a frying pan on a low fire, with onions until they are slightly golden and not burned. As soon as the bacon's fat starts to melt, add a small piece of chili pepper. Add tomato and cook it over a slow flame for 15 minutes.

3 Bring 1 gallon of water to a boil with 4 teaspoons of salt cook the pasta in it, stirring well. While still slightly uncooked, drain the pasta and pour into a large bowl, garnishing it with sauce and the cheese. Mix well before serving.

Wine suggestion:
Colli Picchioni Rosso (see page 163)

Ravioli Di Pesce

Seafood Ravioli

2 large shrimp, cleaned,
   peeled & deveined
3 oz. sole
2 oz. parsley, chopped
2 large scallops
1 clove garlic, chopped
1/4 cup extra virgin olive oil
1/2 stalk of celery, chopped
1 tsp. saffron
2 oz. onion, chopped
3 oz. butter
1 cup fish or vegetable stock
   (see page 28)
3 oz. heavy cream
28 wonton wrappers or
   ravioli dough
salt and pepper to taste
egg wash

1 For Stuffing: In a medium pan, sweat onions, celery and garlic. Add seafood and season with salt and pepper. Add parsley and cook for 3-5 minutes. Remove from heat. Place mixture into a food processor and mix into a paste.

2 For Ravioli Preparation: Lay out wonton wrappers or ravioli dough. Place $\frac{1}{2}$ oz. of seafood mixture into the center of each wonton. Paint the outside edges of the wonton with egg wash. Fold wonton over and press around the edges to seal completely. Boil ravioli in salted water for 2-3 minutes.

3 For Sauce: In a medium saucepan, add butter, stock, saffron, and heavy cream. Cook until mixture is a creamy consistency.

4 To Serve: Drop ravioli into sauce. Toss lightly to coat. Garnish with parsley and oven roasted tomatoes (see page 21) if desired.

Wine suggestion: Chardonnay or one of Marcello's favorites: Sonoma Cutrer (see page 158)

Troppi cuochi guastano la cucina.
English translation: Too many cooks spoil the broth.

Ravioli di Funghi alle Erbe e Parmigiano

Wild Mushroom Ravioli with Herbs & Parmigiano Sauce

Serves 4
(40 Ravioli)

For Stuffing:
5 oz. each of Portobello, Shiitake,
  Oyster and Porcini mushrooms,
  cleaned and diced
4 tbsp. Parmigiano Reggiano
1 oz. butter
1 1/2 oz. extra virgin olive oil
1 medium onion, chopped
salt & pepper to taste

Ravioli Preparation:
40 wonton wrappers or ravioli
dough
egg wash

Butter Parmigiano Herb Sauce:
1 stick of butter
1 fresh plum tomato,
  seeded and diced
2 tbsp. fresh sage, chopped
6 oz. chicken stock (see page 28)
2 tbsp. fresh chives, chopped
2 oz. Parmigiano Reggiano
salt and pepper to taste
some shaved Parmigiano Reggiano
  (for garnish)

1 For Stuffing: Add butter and olive oil into a large fry pan. Sweat onions and add mushrooms. Sauté until cooked through. Remove from heat, add parmigiano. Pass mushroom mixture through food processor until finely minced. Add salt and pepper to taste.

2 For Ravioli Preparation: Lay out wonton wrappers. Place ¹/₂ oz. mushroom mix into center of each wonton. Paint the outside edges of wonton with egg wash. Fold wonton over and press around the edges to seal completely. Cook for 2 minutes in salted, boiling water. Drain and serve with Butter Parmigiano Herb sauce (see below).

3 For Butter Parmigiano Herb Sauce: In a small saucepan, combine butter and sage. Cook it for a few seconds, add chicken stock.

4 To Serve: Lightly toss ravioli in sauce until evenly coated. Add some grated cheese. Place in deep serving dish and garnish with shaved Parmigiano Reggiano and diced tomato.

Wine suggestion: Chianti Classico or one of Marcello's favorites: Chianti Classico Gold Riserva Ruffino (see page 128)

Ravioli con Ripieno di Vegetali e Ricotta

Vegetables Ravioli

Serves 4 entrée portions or
8 appetizer portions (40 ravioli)

For Stuffing:
4 oz. of zucchini, carrots, peas or
   any kind of vegetable, cleaned
   and diced
1 oz. butter
1 1/2 oz. extra virgin olive oil
1 medium onion, chopped
2 oz. fresh chopped parsley
3 oz. parmigiano
3 oz. ricotta cheese
salt and pepper to taste

Ravioli Preparation:
40 wonton wrappers
egg wash

Butter and Herb Sauce:
4 oz. butter
2 plum tomatoes, seeded
   and diced
2 tbsp. fresh sage, chopped
6 oz. vegetable stock
   (see page 28)
2 tbsp. fresh chives, chopped
3 oz. parmigiano
salt & pepper to taste

1 _For Stuffing:_ Add olive oil and butter to large frying pan. Sweat onions and add vegetables. Sauté until cooked through. Remove from heat and add parsley. Salt and pepper to taste.

Pass vegetable mixture through food processor until finely minced, add parmigiano and ricotta.

2 _For Ravioli Preparation:_ Lay out 40 wonton wrappers. Place a little vegetable mix into center of each wonton. Paint the outside edges of wonton with the egg wash. Fold wonton over and press around the edges to seal completely, it will look similar to a half moon.

3 Cook 2 minutes in boiling, salted water. Drain and plate. Serve with Butter and Herb Sauce (see below). Add parmigiano.

4 _For Butter and Herb Sauce:_ Melt butter with stock in saucepan. Add herbs, tomatoes and parmigiano.

Wine suggestion: Sauvignon Blanc or one of Marcello's favorites: Sterling Sauvignon Blanc Napa Valley (see page 159)

Pasta with Cuttlefish or Calamari   Serves 2

8 oz. pasta - linguine,
   capellini or spaghetti
2 cloves garlic, chopped
8 oz. fish, sliced (cuttlefish
   or calamari)
2 oz. extra virgin olive oil
3 oz. sweet cherry tomatoes,
   cut in half
chives or parsley
few capers (optional)
few black olives (optional)
red pepper (optional)

1 In a large sauce pan, saute garlic in olive oil over a low flame until garlic is golden. Turn flame off and add fish. Let water evaporate and return to fire. Cook for 2 minutes. Add tomatoes and cook for only one more minute.

2 Boil pasta in salted water until al dente. Drain, reserving some water. Add pasta to sauce pan with some water. Add the herbs. Add the capers or black olives if desired. If you add capers and olives, salt is not necessary.

3 The sauce of this recipe takes only 5 minutes to cook. You can make the sauce while cooking the pasta.

Wine suggestion: Pinot Grigio or one of Marcello's favorites: Hofstätter Pinot Grigio (see page 140)

Pasta alle Vongole in Bianco

Pasta with White Clam Sauce

Serves 2

8 oz. pasta – linguine,
  capellini or spaghetti
2 oz. extra virgin olive oil
2 cloves garlic, chopped
1 oz. chives or parsley,
  chopped
1 dozen Manila clams
red and/or black pepper
  to taste

1 In a large saucepan, sauté garlic in olive oil over a low flame until garlic is golden brown. Add clams. Cook for 2 minutes until clams are open.

2 In a large pot, boil pasta in salted water until al dente. Drain, reserving some of the water. Add pasta to the saucepan with some of the reserved water. Add the herbs and some extra virgin olive oil. Toss to coat. Serve in a pasta bowl.

Wine suggestion:
Colomba Platino Duca Di Salaparuta (see page 161)

Bombolotti con Pescatrice ai Sapori di Mare e Zafferano

Pasta with Monk Fish, Shell Fish and Saffron Sauce
Serves 4

1 lb. bombolotti pasta or rigatoni
1/4 cup extra virgin olive oil
2 cloves garlic, chopped
4 oz. scallions
1 tbsp. saffron
2 cups fish stock (see page 28)
1 lb. rock shrimp
1 lb. monkfish, cut in small pieces
16 mussels, cleaned
16 clams, cleaned
2 oz. chopped fresh parsley

Wine suggestion: Chardonnay or one of Marcello's favorites: Chardonnay Coppo (see page 157)

1 You can cook fish at the same time as the pasta. In a large pot, bring water to a boil. Add salt and pasta. Cook al dente. Pasta will take 13 minutes.

2 In large saucepan heat, olive oil and garlic. Add monkfish and cook for about 2 minutes. Add mussels and clams and cook for 2 minutes. Add saffron and fish stock. Reduce to $^1/_2$. Add rock shrimp and cook for 2 minutes.

3 Drain pasta. Toss with seafood sauce. Add scallions, fresh parsley and sprinkle with extra virgin olive oil.

Linguine con Rugola, Gamberi e Olive Nere

Linguine with Arugula, Shrimp and Black Gaeta Olives
Serves 4

1 lb. linguine pasta
1 cup fish stock (see page 28)
   or water from pasta
4 oz. arugula
1/4 cup extra virgin olive oil
2 oz. gaeta olives
2 cups tomato sauce (see page 94)
2 cloves garlic, chopped
1/4 cup heavy cream

1 In large pot, bring water to boiling. Add salt and pasta. Cook al dente.

2 In a large saucepan heat olive oil and garlic. Add arugola, rock shrimp and black olives together and cook for about 1 minute. Add tomato sauce, stock (or water from pasta) and heavy cream. Reduce to half.

3 Drain pasta and toss into sauce mixture. Arugula, olives and shrimp should be on top of pasta. This dish must be done quickly as shrimp and arugula should not be overcooked.

Wine suggestion: Vernaccia Di San Gimignano or one of Marcello's favorites: Vernaccia di san Gimignano San Quirico (see page 143)

Trenette con Granchio, Porri e Pomodoretti Arrostiti

Trenette or Linguine Pasta with Crab Meat, Leeks and Oven Roasted Tomato

Serves 4

1 lb. trenette pasta
1 lb. crab meat
2 cloves garlic, chopped
1/4 cup extra virgin olive oil
1 oz. basil, chopped
8 oz. sweet cherry tomatoes
1 cup fish stock (see page 28)
   or water from pasta
1 oz. fresh parsley, chopped
3 oz. chopped leeks

Wine suggestion: Macullan Pino & Toi (see page 161)

1 Set oven at 250°. In a baking pan, place cherry tomatoes, a little olive oil and salt and pepper. Bake in oven for 3 hours. Remove and place in a bowl.

2 In large sauté pan, heat olive oil and garlic and leeks and stir fry for a few minutes. Add fish stock or vegetable stock, crabmeat and oven roasted tomatoes. Cook for 2 minutes and set aside.

3 In a large pot, bring water to a boil. Add salt and pasta. Cook al dente.

4 Drain pasta and toss into sauce. Add basil and parsley (red pepper optional).

5 To serve, place crabmeat on top of pasta; sprinkle with small amount of extra virgin olive oil.

Gnocchi

Potato Dumpling

Serves 4

1 lb. Idaho potatoes
7 oz. all-purpose flour
1 egg
1 oz. parmigiano
pinch of salt

Now you can serve your gnocchi with your favorite sauce.

Options:
- Dust gnocchi with butter, parmigiano and sage.
- Meat Ragu (see page 95)
- Tomato Sauce (see page 94)
- Pesto Sauce (see page 97)
- Puttanesca Sauce (see page 95)

1 Season water with salt to boil potatoes with skin for 50 minutes. Put fork through to check tenderness.

2 On flat surface put flour and form a crater. When potatoes are done cooking, quickly drain and cool off with small amount of water. Potatoes still need to be hot, but not boiling.

3 Peel potatoes and put them through a mash potato press or food mill. Take potatoes and put in middle of flour. Add 1 egg, parmigiano and pinch of salt. Fold potatoes into flour and mix together, but do not overknead.

4 With flour on flat surface roll into cylinders. Cut 1/2" thick diced pieces. With knife, cut into small little pieces and dust with flour to keep from sticking.

5 You can boil gnocchi as they are or make little marks on pasta by rolling with fork. Put gnocchi onto sheet pan. Boil water and drop them into salted water. When gnocchi floats to top they are done, approximately 1 1/2 minutes.

*In Florence you think, in Rome you pray, in Venice you love.
In all three you eat." —Italian Proverb*

Gnocchi Sorrentina

Potato Gnocchi with Tomato and Mozzarella Cheese

For the Gnocchi:
(see previous page)

For the sauce:
1 tsp. hot pepper flakes
4 cups basic tomato sauce
   (see recipe page 94)
1 tsp. Kosher salt or to taste
8 fresh basil leaves
1/2 lb. fresh mozzarella, cut into
   1/4 inch cubes
3 oz. parmigiano cheese
2 oz. olive oil
1 garlic clove, sliced

1 In a sauté pan heat olive oil with garlic and red pepper. Add tomato sauce and some basil and bring to boil.

2 Drop the gnocchi into the boiling water and cook until floating aggressively, 2 to 3 minutes. Carefully transfer the gnocchi to the pan with the sauce using a slotted spoon. Turn the heat to medium and toss gently for about 30 seconds. Tear the basil leaves into a few pieces and add them along with the mozzarella cubes.

3 Toss together for 30 seconds longer, pour into a heated bowl and serve immediately with some parmigiano. Garnish the gnocchi with some basil.

Wine suggestion: Lacrima Christi Rosso Mastroberardino (see page 163)

Egg Pasta
3 eggs, beaten
1 tsp. salt
2 cups all-purpose flour
2 tbsp. water

No Egg Pasta
1 1/2 cups of flour
  (semolina recommended)
1 cup of water
1 tbsp. extra virgin olive oil
1 tbsp. of salt

1 No Egg Pasta: To make pasta combine flour and salt in a mixing bowl. Create a crater in the center and add half cup of water and oil. Begin to work flour toward the center mixing all the ingredients. As pasta begins to form, add remaining water as needed.

1 Egg Pasta: In a medium sized bowl, combine flour and salt. Make a crater in the flour, add the slightly beaten egg and mix. Mixture should form a stiff dough. If needed, stir in 1 to 2 tablespoons water.

2 On a lightly floured surface, knead dough for about 3 to 4 minutes. With a pasta machine or by hand roll dough out to desired thinness. Use machine or knife to cut into strips of desired width.

2 This type of pasta needs to be a little drier than basic pasta. Knead the pasta for a few minutes, cover it and let the pasta rest for 20 minutes.

3 Roll pasta into 1/2" thick sheets trim ends and sides until the pasta roughly resembles a rectangle. Cut into 1 inch-wide strips. Cut each strip crosswise into 1/2" matchstick pieces. Each matchstick piece is ready to be formed into a ciufoli shape.

4 By pressing down firmly with the tip of your finger the pasta edges will curl and form the ciufoli shape. Make sure they are very thin. Put the ciufoli with little semolina on a wood tray or baking pan ready to be cooked.

Risotto ai Funghi

Mushroom Risotto

1 lb. Arborio rice
1 oz. milk or cream
4 oz. butter
12 cups chicken stock
   (see page 28)
2 oz. extra virgin olive oil
1 small onion, diced
2 lbs. mixed mushrooms,
   sliced
1 cup dry white wine
1/2 cup parmigiano, grated

1 In a small pan, sauté mushrooms in 2 oz. of butter and 1 oz. of oil and set aside. In a medium pan, heat the rest of the olive oil and 2 oz. of butter. Add onion and sauté until golden.

2 Add rice and stir for 1 minute. Add red wine let it reduce then add broth a little at a time, stirring occasionally until rice is almost cooked (about 18 minutes).

3 Then add mushrooms and cook 2 more minutes. Remove from heat and add parmigiano and cream. Serve hot.

Wine suggestion: Barolo or one of Marcello's favorites: Vietti Barolo (see page 121)

Risotto Primavera

Risotto with Spring Vegetable

Serves 4

1 lb. Arborio rice
4 oz. butter
2 oz. extra virgin olive oil
1 cup dry white wine
1/2 cup grated parmigiano
1 small onion, diced
12 cups vegetable broth
  (see page 28)
seasonal assorted vegetables
  (zucchini, asparagus, peas)

Wine suggestion:
Pinot Grigio or one of Marcello's favorites:
Pinot Grigio Hofstatter (see page 140)

1 Sauté mixed vegetables in oil and stir fry for 2-3 minutes, until al dente. Season with salt and pepper. Set aside.

2 Heat oil and butter in saucepan, add onion, and fry until golden. Add rice and stir for 1 minute until rice is coated. Add wine and stir for 1 minute. Add broth a little at a time stirring occasionally until rice is almost cooked, about 17 minutes.

3 Add vegetables to the rice, cook for 3 more minutes and rice should be al dente. You can keep this recipe pure vegetarian by adding a little extra virgin olive oil or put a little butter and parmigiano and serve.

Risotto con Spinaci e Pollo Bollito

Risotto with Poached Chicken & Spinach

1 lb. Arborio rice
1 lb. chicken
1 carrot
4 oz. celery
1 onion, cut in half
5 tbsp. olive oil, divided
1 onion, chopped
1 lb. spinach, stems removed, leaves julienned
1/2 cup dry white wine
12 cups simmering chicken stock (see page 28)
3/4 cup grated pecorino romano cheese or parmigiano
1/4 cup parsley, chopped
salt and pepper to taste

Wine suggestion: Pinot Bianco or one of Marcello's favorites: Pinot Bianco Volpe Pasini (see page 141)

1 Poach the chicken with onion halves, carrot, celery, parsley & salt. After 1 hour remove the chicken, strain the broth and put aside. Clean the chicken by removing the bones and skin. Put on the side.

2 In a large saucepan, heat 2 tbsp. olive oil over medium-high heat, add chopped onion. Cook for a minute and add rice, stirring constantly, and cook 1 minute more, making sure rice does not brown. Add wine, stirring constantly and let totally evaporate.

3 When wine is evaporated, begin adding stock ½ cup at a time, letting each evaporate before adding the next addition. This operation will take about 17 minutes.

4 Add chicken and spinach and cook for 3 more minutes and rice should be al dente. Remove from heat and stir in butter, parmigiano and parsley. Serve immediately.

A tavola non si invecchia.
English translation: At the table with good friends
and family you do not become old.

Risotto Milanese con Cappesante e Aceto Balsamico

Risotto Milanese with Scallops & Balsamic Glaze — Serves 6

1 lb. Arborio rice
24 large scallops
4 tbsp. butter
1 small onion, finely chopped
1/2 cup dry white wine
12 cups hot chicken stock
   (see page 28)
1/4 tsp. saffron
2 tbsp. butter
extra 2 tbsp. grated parmigiano
   cheese (optional)

Wine suggestion: Merlot or one of Marcello's favorites: Boscaini (see page 150)

1 Heat 4 tbsp. of butter and 2 tbsp. of olive oil in frying pan. Add the onion and cook until tender. Add rice to pan and stir so that the rice is well coated with the butter.

2 Add wine and 1 cup of hot chicken stock or fish stock. Add saffron. Stir well and bring to a boil. When the stock is almost absorbed, add another cup. Stir well again and bring to a boil.

3 When this stock is almost all absorbed, continue adding 1 cup of stock at a time until rice is al dente. Cooking time is about 17 minutes from the first cup of hot chicken stock that was added. Cook the rice uncovered at this time. Stir in extra butter, parmigiano cheese, salt and pepper. Keep stirring until all the butter has melted.

4 For the scallops: In a non stick pan, pan sear 3 to 4 scallops per person for 2 minutes on each side until they are caramelized and not over cooked.

5 For the balsamic sauce: Reduce to $1/4$ 8 oz. of balsamic vinegar with 3 oz. of sugar. Let it cool and it will became a glaze.

6 To arrange the dish: Put risotto in the middle of a plate and position the scallops into the center as well and drizzle with balsamic glaze.

Fish

Zuppa di Pesce

Seafood Soup

4 oz. calamari
6 oz. monkfish
12 mussels
12 clams
4 shrimp
4 medium scallops
3 cloves garlic, chopped
4 cups fish or vegetable stock
   (see page 28)
1 cup tomato sauce (see page 94)
pinch of saffron
1 cup white wine
flour
1/4 cup extra virgin olive oil
1/4 cup Italian parsley, chopped
salt and pepper to taste

1 In a deep sauce pan, add olive oil and garlic. Dust all fish in flour except the mussels, clams, shrimp and calamari. Add monkfish and scallops to the pan, searing for 30 seconds on each side. Season with salt and pepper.

2 Add wine and let evaporate. Add stock, tomato sauce and saffron.

3 Bring to a boil and then add mussels, clams and calamari. Cook an additional 10 minutes. Two minutes before serving, add shrimp and chopped Italian parsley. Serve with garlic bread (see page 90)

Wine suggestion: Pinot Bianco or one of Marcello's favorites: Masut Da Riva (see page 141)

Cappesante con Ragú di Funghi, Porri e Rughetta

Seared Scallops with Leeks, Arugula and Mushroom Ragu

For 2 entrées or 4 appetizers

1/2 onion
2 leeks, julienne
1/2 lb. shiitake mushroom
3 oz. cherry tomato
3 oz. baby arugula
1/2 cup extra virgin olive oil
12 large sea scallops
salt and pepper to taste

1 Sauté the onion with the oil in a large pan, add leeks, mushroom and tomato. Cook for few minutes. Season with salt and pepper. Keep cooking for a few more minutes. Just before you serve, add baby arugula.

2 For the scallops, add some olive oil, salt and pepper. In a very hot, non-stick pan sear the scallops for a minute on each side. Put the vegetable ragu in a dish and add seared scallops on the plate. Finish it with a drizzle of good extra virgin olive oil.

Wine suggestion: Sauvignon Blanc *or one of Marcello's favorites: Sauvignon Blanc Camelot (see page 159)*

Halibut in Crosta di Patate

Potato Crusted Halibut with Spinach And Herb Vinaigrette   Serves 4

24 oz. halibut fillets,
   cut into 4, 6 oz pieces
24 oven roasted tomatoes
   (see page 21)
2 large whole potatoes, peeled
2 oz. chives, chopped
3 oz. melted butter
2 oz. thyme
2 tbsp. cornstarch
1 oz. red vinegar
2 cloves garlic, chopped
3 oz. extra virgin olive oil
1 lb. baby spinach
salt and pepper to taste

Wine suggestion: Chardonnay or one of Marcello's favorites: Ferrari Carano (see page 157)

1 To prepare the fish: Shred potatoes then squeeze to remove water. Place in a medium bowl. Add melted butter, cornstarch, salt and pepper. Layer potato mixture on top of fish. Cover and refrigerate for 20 minutes.

2 To prepare dressing: In a medium bowl, mix salt, pepper, thyme and chives. Add roasted tomatoes, red vinegar, and olive oil. Mix thoroughly and set aside.

3 To sauté the spinach: In a medium pan, heat olive oil and garlic. Stir-fry spinach for 3-4 minutes. Season with salt and pepper and set aside.

4 To sauté the fish: In a non-stick pan, heat olive oil until very hot. Place fish, potato side down in the oil. Let sit for 30 seconds. If desired, place a small amount of butter on top of fish. Place pan in a 400°F oven and bake for 10 minutes.

5 To assemble: Place warm spinach in the middle of plate. Put fish, potato side up (potato should be very crispy) on top of spinach. Drizzle vinegar dressing around the plate.

Cernia con Peperoni, Capperi, Olive Nere e Pomodoro

Grouper with Sweet Peppers, Capers, Black Olives & Tomato Sauce

Serves 4

24 oz. of Grouper cut into small cubes
8 large Sea scallops
2 yellow peppers
2 red peppers
2 oz. of capers
2 oz. of black calamata or gaeta olives
1 small onion
8 oz. of San Marzano plum
   Italian tomatoes
2 cloves of garlic
1 oz. basil
2 oz. chopped Italian parsley
1/2 cup extra virgin olive oil
salt and pepper to taste

1 In a sautée pan, cook onions, garlic and peppers with oil for 4 minutes. Add salt, pepper, tomatoes, basil, capers and black olives. Cook for ten minutes.

2 Pan sear fish and then bake it for 10 minute at 375° to serve place fish on a plate put the sauce next to it. Add chopped parsley and serve it with baked or grilled polenta (see page 89).

Wine suggestion: White blend or Pinot Grigio or one of Marcello's favorites: Colomba Platino Duca Di Salaparuta (see page 161)

Salmone in Crosta di Ravanello

Salmon with Horseradish Crust and Mustard Sauce

4 pieces of salmon (8 oz. each)
1/4 cup olive oil to cook the salmon

For the crust:
4 tbsp. horseradish
2 tbsp. dijon mustard
1 cup Japanese panco bread-
    crumbs or plain bread crumbs

For the sauce:
pepper, optional
1/2 cup white wine
1/2 cup heavy cream
4 tbsp. dijon mustard
chopped tomatoes
chopped chives

1 Mix together the horseradish with the 2 tbsp. of mustard, and spread on top of the salmon. Then put the breadcrumbs on top of that. Heat oil in a skillet, and when very hot, put in salmon crust side down, and sear for 10 seconds, turn over and sear other side for 10 more seconds. Put the fish in a baking pan that has a little oil. Bake for about 12 minutes without turning at 400°.

2 Sauce: In a medium saucepan, reduce the wine by half. Then add cream and the 4 tbsp. of mustard. Bring to a boil, then simmer for 4 minutes until smooth.

3 To serve: Put salmon on the plate and spoon the sauce around it. Garnish with chopped tomatoes and chives.

Wine suggestion: Chardonnay or one of Marcello's favorites: Chardonnay Robert Mondavi (see page 157)

Gamberi con Zucchine Fagioli e Frutti di Mare

Shrimp with Zucchini Cannellini Beans and Shell Fish   Serves 2

8 medium-large shrimp, cleaned
16 mussels, cleaned
16 manila clams, cleaned
1 zucchini, diced in small cubes
2 cups cooked cannellini beans
  with liquid
2 cloves garlic, sliced
1 cup tomato sauce (see page 94)
1/2 cup white wine
1/4 cup olive oil
pinch red pepper
salt and pepper to taste
6 leaves of fresh basil, chopped

1 In a sauté pan heat oil, add garlic and cook until brown. Remove from heat, add zucchini and shell fish. Bring back to fire. Cover and cook for 30 seconds then remove cover and add beans with liquid, wine, red pepper and tomato sauce.

2 Now add shrimp and chopped fresh basil and cook for 3 more minutes and serve. Shrimp should not be over cooked.

Wine suggestion: Zinfandell or one of Marcello's favorites: Primitivo le Corte (see page 152)

Filetti di Sogliola al Prosecco con Giardiniera di Vegetali

Filet of Sole, Prosecco Wine Sauce and Mixed Vegetables   Serves 2

For the fish:
4 filet of lemon sole
    (about 3 oz. each or any sole)
4 tbsp. olive oil
2 oz. flour

For the vegetable:
4 tbsp. of extra virgin olive oil
1/4 of onion, chopped
2 asparagus, diced
1 small zucchini, diced
1/4 cup poached fresh or frozen peas
1 tomato, diced
1/4 cup red roasted peppers, diced
    (see page 87)
1/4 cup roasted yellow peppers,
    diced (see page 87)
1 oz. chopped parsley

Wine suggestion: Prosecco or one
of Marcello's favorites: Prosecco Mionetto
(see page 137)

1 In a sauté pan, heat oil. Dust the filet of sole with flour and cook in the oil for 1 minute on each side. Remove the sole and put aside.

2 Clean and use the same pan in which you have cooked the fish. Heat the oil add onion and cook for a minute then add the rest of the vegetables. Season to your taste then add Prosecco and butter.

3 Reduce for a minute, add stock and cream (optional) then put fish back in the pan with the sauce. Cook for one more minute sprinkle with some chopped parsley and serve hot.

For the sauce:
8 oz. of prosecco wine
pinch white pepper
salt to taste
2 oz. butter
1 oz. heavy cream, optional
2 oz. vegetable stock (see page 28)

Meat

Pollo con Salsiccia, Peperoni e Aceto Balsamico

Breast of Chicken with Sweet Peppers, Italian Sausage and Balsamic Sauce

Serves 2

14 oz. chicken breast
8 oz. italian sausage
1 small yellow pepper
1 small red pepper
1/2 small onion
3 oz. balsamic vinegar
1 clove garlic
fresh rosemary
flour
4 oz. chicken stock (see page 28)
2 oz. fresh parsley
4 oz. olive oil
salt and pepper to taste

1 Cut the chicken into small cubes, 1 inch long, and do the same for the peppers and the onions.

2 Bake the sausage for 10 minutes so it is still very juicy. Let it rest and then cut up the sausage the same as the chicken. Heat olive oil in a sauté pan. Add onions, peppers and chopped garlic.

3 Stir-fry for 3 minutes, and then add the chicken that has been floured and the sausage. Cook for 5 minutes then add salt and pepper to taste. At the last minute add balsamic vinegar and reduce. Add chicken stock, cook 1 more minute, add fresh parsley and serve with garlic bread (see page 90).

Wine suggestion: Illuminati Lumen (see page 163)

Pollo Ripieno

Stuffed Breast of Chicken with Veal and Spinach

1 lb. veal for stew
1 carrot, chopped
1 celery stalk, chopped
1 onion, chopped
8 oz. white wine
1 lb. spinach
8 oz. parmigiano
8 oz. ricotta cheese
4 oz. olive oil
4 large breast of chicken
4 oz. brown stock (see page 96)
truffle oil
salt and pepper to taste

Wine suggestion: Barolo or one
of Marcello's favorites: Barolo Vietti
(see page 121)

1 Sautéed the veal in olive oil and add the vegetables. When well roasted add white wine, salt and pepper. Cook slowly in the oven at 375° for one hour until veal is tender. Put veal mix in a food processor and add ricotta, parmigiano and poached spinach, well drained.

2 Flatten the breast of chicken, put stuffing in the middle and fold. Flour the chicken and sauté in a non-stick pan. Bake the chicken in the oven at 350° for 20 minutes.

3 At that time you add to the chicken $1/2$ glass of white wine, let it reduce for a few minutes, add the brown stock, cook for 5 more minutes and remove from oven. Serve chicken in a plate, pour sauce over top and drizzle with truffle oil.

Petti di Pollo in Crosta di Pignoli e Glassa di Marsala

Pignoli Crusted Chicken with Raisins, Sweet Peppers and Marsala Glaze

Serves 4

1 1/2 lbs. chicken breast
1 cup marsala wine
1/4 cup of sugar
1/2 cup dry raisins
1 cup pignoli nuts, crushed
1 large yellow pepper, julienned
1 large red pepper, julienned
1 onion, julienned
1/4 lb. salted butter
1/4 cup olive oil
fresh parsley, chopped
2 egg whites
salt and pepper to taste

1 Soak raisins in hot water and set aside. Lightly flour the chicken, season with salt and pepper, dip in egg whites, then dust with crushed pignoli nuts. Sauté the chicken in butter, crust side down for about 30 seconds on each side. Set aside.

2 In a separate pan, sauté onions and peppers in olive oil. Add drained raisins and the rest of the pignoli nuts. Add salt and pepper to taste and continue sautéing until well cooked for about 10 minutes.

3 Place chicken in a 450° oven and cook for 10 minutes. To serve, place chicken on plate, top with onion mixture and sprinkle with fresh parsley.

4 For Marsala glaze: Reduce 1 cup of marsala wine with $1^{1}/_{4}$ cups of sugar to half. When cold it will become like a syrup. Drizzle this on top of chicken.

Wine suggestion:
Terre d'Agala (see page 163)

Bistecca al Ginepro

Hanger Steak with Juniper Berry Sauce

Serves 10

5 lbs. Hanger Steak

Marinade:
8 oz. fresh tarragon
1 clove garlic, minced
3 oz. honey
1 cup balsamic vinegar
2 cups extra-virgin olive oil
salt and pepper to taste

Juniper Berry Sauce:
8 oz. juniper berries
3 pieces shallots, minced
2 qt. port wine
1 qt. brown stock (see page 96)
salt and pepper to taste

1 Marinade: Mix honey, balsamic vinegar and olive oil together. Add tarragon and garlic, salt and pepper to taste. Place hanger steak in marinade and refrigerate for 2-3 hours. Grill steak to your favorite temperature.

2 Sauce: Sear the shallots in olive oil until golden. Add the port wine and brown stock and reduce to half. Salt and pepper to taste. Arrange slice steak on a plate and drizzle with the sauce.

Wine suggestion: Super Tuscan or one of Marcello's favorites: Corbaia Castello Di Bossi (see page 131)

Involtini di Vitello

Veal Rollatini

Serves 4

1 lb. veal cutlets,
   cut into 12 scaloppinis
12 small pieces of prosciutto
12 small pieces of mozzarella
   or fontina cheese
3 oz. flour
1 cup white wine
1/4 cup extra virgin olive oil
3 oz. butter
1/2 lb. mushrooms, sliced
1 cup chicken stock
   (see page 28)
salt and pepper to taste

1 Lay veal scaloppini on cutting board. Fill with prosciutto and cheese. Roll scaloppini up and then roll in flour. Close with a toothpick.

2 In a sauté pan, add oil and butter, and pan sear veal until golden brown. Set aside. Add a little more oil and butter to the pan and sauté mushrooms for a few minutes.

3 Add white wine, cook until it evaporates. Add chicken stock, reduce down to one half. Add 2 tbsp. butter. Place veal in ovenproof pan, cover with sauce. Bake at 450° for 5 minutes.

Wine suggestion: Chardonnay or one of Marcello's favorites: Cervaro della Sala Antinori (see page 158)

Cotolette di Vitello Estive

Veal Estive

1 lb. veal cutlets
4 eggs, beaten
plain bread crumbs
2 oz. flour
2 oz. butter
pinch of oregano
10 leaves of basil
1/2 cup extra virgin olive oil
6 ripe tomatoes, cut into
   small cubes
1lb. fresh mozzarella, cut into
   small cubes
salt and pepper to taste

1 Bread cutlets. First flour, next eggs, then breadcrumbs. Set aside.

2 Put tomatoes and mozzarella in a bowl. Add oregano and basil. Salt and pepper to taste. Add extra virgin olive oil. Mix together. Set aside.

3 Pan fry veal cutlets in butter and extra virgin olive oil. When cooked, drain on paper towel. Place veal cutlets in baking pan and top with tomato/mozzarella mixture.

4 Broil for 1 minute. Serve with roasted potatoes. *Variation: In the summer, this dish can be served at room temperature with no broiling necessary.

Wine suggestion: Pinot Grigio or one of Marcello's favorites: Maso Canali (see page 139)

Braised Veal Shank   Serves 6

6 pieces of tied Ossobuco
 (veal shank)
1 cup onion, diced
3 cloves garlic, minced
chopped parsley
3/4 cup diced celery
3/4 cup diced carrot
4 cups chicken stock (see page 28)
1 cup dry white wine
2 strips of lemon peel
1 1/2 cups of San Marzano
 plum Italian tomatoes,
 chopped with juice
1/2 cup vegetable oil
fresh thyme, basil and bay leaves
salt and pepper to taste

Wine suggestion:
Brunello Di Montalcino or one of
Marcello's favorites: Villa Banfi Brunello
Di Montalcino (see page 129)

1 Preheat oven to 350.° Add some vegetable oil to large covered pot over medium heat and sweat the onion, carrots and celery until lightly browned. Add lemon peel and garlic and remove from heat. Place vegetables in large casserole.

2 Add oil to sauté pan over medium-high heat and brown the veal shanks on all sides. Stand the veal on top of the browned vegetables.

3 Remove any excess fat from the sauté pan and turn the heat to high. Deglaze the pans with white wine, scraping any caramelized bits from the bottom of the pan. Strain this liquid over the veal.

4 In the same sauté pan, bring chicken broth to a simmer and pour into the casserole. Add chopped tomatoes and thyme, basil and bay leaves. Season with salt and pepper. The liquid should just barely cover the meat.

5 Bring to a simmer on top of the stove and cover tightly. Place in oven for 1 1/2 to 2 hours, basting every 20 minutes. Carefully turn the veal once during cooking.

6 To serve: Carefully remove veal from pot. Remove string and set aside. Return the pot to the heat. Skim any scum that may have risen to the top and reduce the braising liquid to concentrate the flavors. Check and adjust the seasoning. Add chopped parsley.

7 Place one veal shank on warmed plate and ladle some of the braising liquid and vegetables on. (If liquid is too thin, puree the vegetables and add chicken stock and cornstarch to thicken.)

The traditional accompaniment for Ossobuco is Risotto Milanese (see page 56).

Costolette d'Agnello con Cime di Rape

Lamb Chops with Broccoli Rabe

16 lamb chops, center cut
1 1/2 lbs. broccoli rabe,
  without stems
12 cloves garlic, crushed
3 stalks fresh rosemary
1 cup extra virgin olive oil
salt to taste
red pepper flakes to taste

Wine suggestion: Montepulciano
D'Abruzzo or one of Marcello's favorites:
Don Luigi Di Maio Norante from Molise
Region (see page 134)

1 Marinate lamb chops in $^1/_2$ cup olive oil, 8 cloves of garlic and fresh rosemary for 3 hours.

2 Steam broccoli rabe for a few minutes, drain and set aside. Put $^1/_2$ cup olive oil in frying pan. Fry lamb chops on a high heat until chops are crispy and cooked pink. Set aside.

3 In the same oil, add 4 cloves of garlic and cook until golden. Add broccoli rabe, salt and red pepper flakes to taste. Arrange chops on plate in a circle with broccoli rabe in the middle. Sprinkle with a little extra virgin olive oil.

Agnello in Crosta di Pane alle Erbe e Aglio

Rack of Lamb with Garlic Herb Bread Crust & Wine Sauce   Serves 4

4 individual racks of domestic
    or imported lamb
salt and pepper to taste
1 oz. rosemary
2 cloves garlic, chopped
1 oz. oregano
1 oz. chopped parsley
2 cup plain breadcrumbs
1/4 cup extra virgin olive oil
4 tbsp. Dijon mustard
1 cup white wine
1 cup brown stock (see page 96)

Wine suggestion: Super Tuscan or
one of Marcello's favorites: Biondi Santi
Sassoalloro (see page 130)

1 Take a rack of lamb ready to be cooked and season with salt and pepper.

2 In a sauté pan heat some oil and sear the lamb for 2 minutes on each side. Remove from pan and spread some mustard on top of the lamb.

3 In a bowl mix breadcrumbs, parsley, oregano, garlic, rosemary, oil and mix well. Put some of the breadcrumb mixture on top of the lamb and bake in a preheated oven at 400° for 12 minutes.

4 Now add the wine to the pan and let evaporate for about a minute, then add the brown stock and let cook for 2 more minutes. The lamb should be cooked pink. Let the lamb rest for 10 minutes before serving. The lamb should be lukewarm and the sauce hot.

Ossobuco d'Agnello con Funghi

Lamb Shanks with Mushroom Ragu

Serves 4

4 lamb shanks
Kosher salt and freshly
  ground pepper
3/4 lb. mixed fresh mushrooms
  (such as shiitake, Portobello,
  chanterelle, dry porcini) roughly
  chopped
1 tbsp. minced garlic
1 cup diced onion (1/4 inch diced)
1/2 cup diced carrot (1/4 inch diced)
1/2 cup diced celery (1/4 inch diced)
2 cups dry red wine
1 bay leaf
3 cups chicken stock (see page 28)
3 cups tomatoes, peeled, seeded
  and chopped
3 tbsp. finely chopped fresh basil
1 tbsp. oregano, finely chopped
1/2 cup olive oil

*Wine suggestion: Super Tuscan or
one of Marcello's favorites: Col Di Sasso
Banfi (see page 130)*

1 Preheat the oven to 300°F. Heat half of the olive oil in a baking pan. Season the shanks with salt and pepper and brown on all sides, about 10 minutes. Remove to a plate.

2 In the same baking pan, add the remaining olive oil and the garlic and sauté briefly until light brown. Add the onion, carrots, and celery and season with salt and pepper. Sauté until light brown, about 8 minutes. Bring the shank back in the pan with the vegetables and add mushrooms. Cook for a few minutes.

3 Add the wine and bay leaf, bring to a boil over high heat and cook until it is reduced by half. Add the stock and tomatoes and bring to a boil again. Place meat in the oven to braise until fork tender. Test at 2 hours, but the shanks may take as long as 4 hours.

4 Let the meat cool in the liquid to room temperature. Remove from the braising liquid and reserve separately. Skim off and discard the fat from the braising liquid. Sauce should not be too loose or too thick. You can cook this dish one or two days ahead. The meat will have much more flavor. You can serve this dish with risotto, mash potatoes or pasta.

Filetto di Bue all'Aceto Balsamico

Filet Mignon with Balsamic Vinegar Reduction

4 filets of 8 oz. each
1/4 cup extra virgin olive oil
1 cup balsamic vinegar
1/4 cup sugar
2 oz. salted butter, optional
2 oz. brown stock (see page 96)
salt and pepper to taste

Wine suggestion: Barolo or one of
Marcello's favorites: Barolo Pio Cesare
(see page 121)

1 For sauce: Simmer balsamic vinegar with sugar until reduced by $1/4$. Vinegar should be thick and of syrup consistency. Add brown stock to balsamic reduction and set aside.

2 Marinate the filets with olive oil for a few hours. Grill 5 minutes on each side to medium rare. Set aside.

3 This recipe can be served with Garlic Mashed Potatoes (see page 88) and Cipolline Glassate (see page 84).

Fegato alla Veneziana con Pinoli

Calves Liver with Onions and Pignoli Nuts

Serves 4

1 1/2 lbs. of calves' liver
2 large onions
1/2 cup oil
3 oz. butter
3 oz. pignoli nuts
3 oz. chopped parsley
salt and pepper to taste

1 Cut the calves' liver into thin, not very long strips. Finely slice two large onions, cover and cook onions slowly in oil and butter until golden.

2 Add the liver and the pignoli nuts and cook for 5 to 6 minutes. Add salt to taste. Add chopped, fresh parsley and serve with polenta (see recipe 89).

Wine suggestion: Zinfandel or one of Marcello's favorites: Zinfandel Ravenswood (see page 152)

Cavolo Ripieno di Carne con Pomodoro

Stuffed Cabbage with Meat Baked in Tomato Sauce Serves 6

4 oz. ground beef
4 oz. ground veal
2 eggs
1 oz. chopped garlic
3 oz. parmigiano
1 oz. chopped parsley
1 onion, chopped
6 leaves of fresh basil
12 leaves of savoy cabbage
1/2 cup extra virgin olive oil
4 cups tomato sauce (see page 94)
3 slices of white bread, no crust,
    soaked in milk and squeezed
1/2 glass white wine
2 cups chicken stock (see page 28)
salt and pepper to taste

1 Mix the meat with eggs, salt, pepper, parmigiano, parsley, garlic and bread. Mix together. Take a little bit of the meat, pan fry it quickly and taste for flavor. Set aside.

2 Take savoy cabbage leaves, poach them in salty water for 1 minute. Remove from water and place on paper towel to dry.

3 Scoop some of the meat and put in the middle of each cabbage leaf. Fold to create a little pocket and roll up tight. You can tie with string to keep it tight if you'd like.

4 Put olive oil in saute pan and add chopped onion, cook for a few minutes. Dust each cabbage roll with flour and cook with onion for 1 minute on each side. Add the wine, let evaporate, add tomatoes, chicken stock and basil. Transfer the cabbage into a baking pan and bake for 1 hour at 375°.

5 When done, spoon sauce over cabbage. The sauce should not be too thick or too loose. Can be served as appetizer or entree.

Mangiare per vivere e non vivere per mangiare.
English translation: Eat to live and not live to eat

Bistecca alla Fiorentina

Grilled Porterhouse Steak Florentine Style

Serves 2

2 lb. Porterhouse steak,
  about 2 inches thick
kosher salt
coarse ground black pepper
extra virgin olive oil
1 lemon

Wine suggestion:
Chianti or one of Marcello's
favorites: Castello di Bossi
Classico Berardo (see page 127)

1 Let the steak rest outside of the refrigerator for one hour before cooking. Liberally season the steak with salt and pepper and press the seasoning into the meat.

2 To grill: Charcoal will be ideal for cooking this meat otherwise you can use a hot, clean grill. Grill the steak for about 5-6 minutes on each side for medium rare. Move the steak every two minutes or so for even cooking and a crispy exterior.

3 Remove the steak to a carving board and let rest for at least 5 minutes before slicing. Cut the lemon in half and brush on top of the steak and sprinkle with olive oil. Serve with roasted potatoes and sautéed spinach (see page 90).

Anitra con Caponata di Melanzane

Duck Breast with Sweet and Sour Eggplant

Serves 4

4 duck breasts
salt and pepper to taste
1/4 cup balsamic vinegar
1/4 cup extra virgin olive oil
2 cloves of slice garlic

1 Take the skin off the duck and season the duck with salt and pepper. Marinate the duck with balsamic vinegar, olive oil and garlic for 12 hours. Grill the duck pink for 2 minutes on each side.

2 At the same time, warm up some caponata (see page 13). Put caponata in a dish, slice the duck and serve with caponata.

Wine suggestion: *Nero D'avola or one of Marcello's favorites:*
Duca Enrico Di Salaparuta (see page 136)

Quaglie con Salvia Prosciutto al Vino Bianco

Quail Wrapped in Prosciutto with Sage & White Wine Sauce   Serves 4

8 boneless quails split in half
16 slices of Italian prosciutto
6 leaves of sage
5 oz. unsalted butter
1 cup dry white wine
1/2 cup chicken stock (see page 28)
1/2 cup brown stock, optional
   (see page 96)
1/4 cup olive oil

Wine suggestion:
Brunello Di Montalcino or one of
Marcello's favorites: Villa Banfi (see page 129)

1 Take half of each quail and season with a little salt and black pepper. Wrap with prosciutto and repeat with the rest of the bird.

2 In a sauté pan, heat some oil with 2 oz. of butter and sage, then dust the quail with some flour. Cook for 1 minute on each side on a slow flame and remove. Place quail in a baking pan.

3 In the same pan add wine, stock and butter and cook to reduce. Sauce should be creamy. Bake quail for 10 minutes at 400°. Serve with some of the wine sauce and baked or grilled polenta (see page 89).

Struzzo in Salsa Mediterranea

Ostrich with Mediterranean Sauce   Serves 4

24 oz. ostrich meat (from the fan)
1/2 cup extra-virgin olive oil
salt and pepper to taste

Underline For Sauce:
2 hot cherry peppers with seeds
   removed
2 sweet cherry peppers with
   seeds removed
2 oz. capers
3 oz. sun-dried tomato
3 oz. black olives
3 cloves garlic
1 cup extra-virgin olive oil
1 tbsp. chives
1 tbsp. parsley

1 Brush ostrich with olive oil. Grill 3 minutes on each side to medium-rare (ostrich is best cooked to medium-rare). Set aside.

2 Chop very fine by hand, or in a food processor, the cherry and sweet peppers, capers, sun-dried tomatoes, olives & garlic. Add the olive oil, chives and parsley and mix until fully combined.

3 Slice ostrich and drizzle with Mediterranean sauce. Serve with mesclun salad.

Wine suggestion: Riesling or one of Marcello's favorites:
Riesling Hogue (see page 160)

Coniglio Arrosto con Erbe

Roasted Baby Rabbit with Herbs
Serves 4

1 1/2 lbs. rabbit
sage
rosemary
1 clove garlic
2 cup wine vinegar
3 oz. olive oil
salt and pepper to taste

Wine suggestion:
Chianti or one of Marcello's favorites: Rocca delle Macie Chianti Classico (see page 128)

1 Cut the rabbit into small pieces. Wash and dry. Chop a few sage leaves, a sprig of rosemary and garlic. Mix herbs with salt and pepper and rub the pieces of rabbit in the herbs and place in a deep dish. Mix together vinegar and 6 tbsp. olive oil and pour over the rabbit. Marinate for 24 hours, turning the meat occasionally so that it absorbs the flavors.

2 Pour the marinade and rabbit into a saucepan and cook covered over low heat oven at 350° for about 45 minutes. Uncover the pot, turn up the heat to 450° and cook for another 10 minutes or until the rabbit is tender and the juice is almost completely reduced. Serve with baked polenta (see page 89).

Falso Magro

Stuffed Beef Sicilian Style
Serves 4

1 1/2 lbs. beef rib, blade meat
  (or beef chuck shoulder)
7 oz. prosciutto
7 oz. sausage
1 slice pancetta
3/4 lb. lean ground beef
3 oz. fresh Pecorino
2 eggs
4 hard boiled eggs
1 clove garlic
6 slices crust less bread (soaked
  in milk and squeezed dry)
1 onion, chopped
1 bunch parsley
2 oz. strutto (lard)
1 cup red wine
2 cups crushed tomato
1 tbsp. tomato paste
2 cups of warm water
salt and pepper to taste

1 Pound the meat until it is 1/4" thick. Prepare the stuffing: chop the prosciutto, sausage and pancetta and mix with the ground beef. Add grated Pecorino, 2 eggs, chopped garlic and parsley, bread, salt and pepper. Mix thoroughly to achieve a smooth mixture. Hard boil the remaining eggs and remove the shells. Spread the meat filling into the pounded steak and place whole, hard boiled eggs in the middle. Roll up the meat and tie securely.

2 Brown the chopped onion in lard in a frying pan. Add the meat roll and brown on all sides. Splash with red wine. When the wine has evaporated, add the tomato pulp and paste diluted with 1 cup of warm water. Add salt and pepper and cook in the oven at 400° for 1 hour and 10 minutes basting occasionally so that the top does not get dry. Remove the meat from the roasting pan. Let cool, strain the cooking juices, adjust seasoning and serve over the sliced beef roll.

Wine suggestion:
Nero D'Avola or one of Marcello's favorites: Planeta Santa Cecilia (see page 136)

Vegetables

Side dishes

Gratin of Asparagus with Parmigiano

Serves 2

10 asparagus
4 tbsp. Parmigiano Reggiano
  cheese, grated
1/2 cup chicken stock (see page 28)
  or water
2 oz. butter

1 Clean asparagus and poach in salted water. Cook until al dente.

2 In separate sauté pan over low heat, add butter and chicken stock. Allow butter to melt slowly. Add asparagus and 2 tbsp. parmigiano. Let cook for 1 minute until sauce is creamy.

3 Put on plate and top with remaining parmigiano. Place plate under broiler for 30 seconds to brown and crisp. Serve it right away.

Wine suggestion: Pinot Bianco or one of Marcello's favorites: Pinot Bianco Volpe Pasini (see page 141)

Involtini di Melanzane con Ripieno di Funghi e Fontina

Eggplant Rollatini Filled with Mushroom Ricotta & Fontina   Serves 4

8 slices of 1/4" thick eggplant, sliced vertically
2 cup vegetable oil
2 oz. flour
2 eggs
1 lb. bottom or cremini mushrooms
8 oz. ricotta cheese
2 oz. fontina cheese, diced small
8 slices of fontina cheese
2 oz. parmigiano, for the stuffing
2 oz. parmigiano, to sprinkle
1/2 cup olive oil
1/2 onion, chopped
2 oz. parsley, chopped
1 oz. butter
3 cups tomato sauce (see page 94)
salt and pepper to taste

1 Dust the eggplant in flour then dip in egg and fry eggplant for 20 seconds on each side. Put on paper towel to drain.

2 In saute pan, cook onions and mushrooms for 2-3 minutes. Season with salt and pepper and put mushroom mix into food processor. Add ricotta, parmigiano cheese and small cubes of fontina cheese. Add chopped parsley and put mixture into container.

3 Lay eggplant on cutting board and add stuffing mixture onto eggplant and roll it. Place eggplant in baking pan that has been buttered. Add tomato sauce on top and bake for 15 minutes at 400°.

4 After 15 minutes, take out of oven and place 1 slice of Fontina cheese on top of each eggplant. Bake for 2 more minutes and serve as an appetizer or on top of plain pasta and sprinkle with parmigiano cheese.

Wine suggestion: Dolcetto d'Alba or one of Marcello's favorites: Villadoria Dolcetto d'Alba (see page 124)

Melanzane Ripiene con Purée di Vegetali

Stuffed Eggplant with Vegetables   Serves 6

6 Italian eggplants
1/4 cup olive oil
1/2 onion, chopped
2 peppers, diced
2 zucchini, diced
1/4 cup parmigiano
1/2 cup ricotta
2 oz. parsley
salt and pepper to taste

Wine suggestion:
Sauvignon Blanc (see page 159)

1 Take baby Italian eggplant and cut in half. With a spoon remove the inside and put on the side.

2 Season the eggplant bottom with salt and pepper. In a sauté pan, add olive oil when hot. Sauté the onions, eggplant, peppers & zucchini.

3 Season it well and cook it for five minutes. When cooked, put the vegetable in a food processor. Add Parmigiano, ricotta and parsley to taste. Let the stuffing cool off.

4 Take the stuffing and fill the eggplant bottom. Add a little parmigiano cheese on top. Bake it at 325° for 35 minutes. Enjoy the eggplant as a side to a fish or meat dish or by itself with tomato sauce.

Cipolline Glassate

Glazed Baby Onions   Serves 4

1/3 cup butter
12-14 large cipolline onions
2 tbsp. brown sugar
1 cup water (or other liquid)

1 Peel and core the cipolline onions. Melt butter in large baking dish. Place cipolline onions in dish, cored side up and put brown sugar. Add liquid to dish, cover with foil, and bake 45 minutes at 350°. Remove foil and bake until tender. Syrup will form to spoon over the cipolline onions. Serve in warm baking dish by itself or as a garnish to meat or fish dishes.

Cipolline is an Italian pearl onion known for its flat, saucer-like shape. Previously produced only in Italy, these unusual and elegant onions are now grown in different countries. Cipolline range from 1" to 3" in diameter and are available year-round in most supermarkets. The taste of cooked cipolline is uniquely mild and sweet.

Melanzane alla Parmigiana

Eggplant Parmigiana   Serves 6

2 large eggplants
3 tbsp. of salt
2 beaten eggs
1/2 cup flour
oil for frying
4 cups tomato sauce
   (see page 94)
1 lb. mozzarella cheese,
   sliced or chopped
1/2 cup parmigiano cheese,
   grated

1 Cut the eggplant into $1/2$ inch slices. Sprinkle both sides of each slice with salt, lay out on the plates or tray and let stand for 30-60 minutes. Wash off the salt and immediately pat each slice dry.

2 Heat $1/2$" of oil in the frying pan and cover plates or tray with several layers of paper towels. Put the eggs in one bowl and coat each slice of eggplant with flour and then egg.

3 Fry a single layer of eggplant slices until golden, turn and fry the other side. When the eggplant is tender, transfer to the paper towels and turn to remove excess oil. Repeat with remaining slices, adding more oil to pan as needed. Preheat oven to 350°.

4 Cover the bottom of the baking dish with a few spoonfuls of tomato sauce. We need to create 3 to 4 layers. Sprinkle each layer with some of the mozzarella, parmigiano, few leaves of basil and tomato sauce. Repeat the operation 3 or 4 times, add the remaining sauce and top it with the rest of the mozzarella. Bake for 30 minutes, until heated through and bubbly.

Portobelli Trifolati

Sauteed Portobello with Garlic & Extra Virgin Olive Oil   Serves 4

4 medium portobello mushrooms,
   sliced very thin
1/2 cup extra virgin olive oil
6 cloves of garlic, crushed
1/2 cup chopped Italian parsley
salt and pepper to taste

1 In a saute pan, add oil and garlic. Cook garlic until golden then add portobello. Stir fry for a few minutes then add salt, pepper and parsley. You can serve the mushrooms as an appetizer or with meat or fish.

Ragu di Ceci, Porri Funghi e Spinaci

Chickpeas, Leeks, Mushroom and Baby Spinach Ragú
Serves 6

1 onion, chopped
8 oz. of leeks cut in small cubes
1 lb. chickpeas
8 oz. shiitake mushroom
1 lb. baby spinach
salt and pepper to taste
1/2 cup extra virgin olive oil

You can accompany many types of fish or meat with this vegetable ragu.

1 In sauté pan heat oil, add onions and leeks. Stir-fry for few minutes. Add mushrooms and cook for few more minutes, add salt and pepper.

2 If you use canned chickpeas, add chick peas with liquid. If you use dry chickpeas you need to soak them overnight and cook them for one-hour. Season chickpeas at the end and save some liquid.

3 Now you can add baby spinach. Cook for 1 minute and the ragu is ready to be served. You can pan sear many fish or meat and put on top of the ragu. Drizzle some extra virgin olive oil and serve.

Insalata di Ceci e Cuori di Palma

Chickpeas and Palm Heart Salad
Serves 8

28 ounce can chickpeas,
   drained and rinsed
3/4 cup celery, very thinly sliced
1/2 red onion, minced
10 oz. palm heart, diced small
3 oz. cherry tomatoes, cut in half
3 tbsp. minced fresh Italian parsley
1 clove garlic, very finely minced
1/2 cup extra-virgin olive oil
salt and pepper to taste

1 In a large bowl, stir the chickpeas, palm heart, celery, onion, tomato, parsley, garlic and oil. Season to taste with salt and pepper. Serve immediately.

Peperoni Arrostiti

Roasted Peppers

Serves 4-6

3 cloves garlic, sliced
2 large red bell peppers
2 large yellow bell peppers
1/3 cup extra virgin olive oil
1 teaspoon salt

1 Preheat the oven to 450°. Place the peppers, with their stems intact, on a baking sheet or in a roasting pan, and roast 20-30 minutes, or until the skins darken and blister.

2 Remove the peppers from the oven, and place them in a paper bag. Close the bag by folding over twice. Set the peppers aside to cool.

3 Take the peppers from the bag and remove the skins, stems, and seeds. If necessary, rinse the peppers to make peeling easier. Cut the peppers into strips.

4 Add sliced garlic, salt and extra virgin olive oil. You can serve this as an appetizer or to accompany many other dishes.

Carciofi e Patate alla Molisana

Artichoke and Potato from Molise

Serves 4

16 baby artichokes
4 small potatoes
1 onion, sliced
salt and pepper to taste
1/4 cup extra virgin olive oil
1 oz. red pepper
chopped parsley
2 oz. pancetta

1 Clean artichokes and cut in half. Put in cold water with lemon. Peel potatoes, cut into quarters and put in water.

2 Boil water and poach potatoes for 6 minutes or until al dente. Drain and put aside. Drain artichokes and dry them.

3 In a sauté pan, heat oil and cook onions for 2 minutes. Add artichokes and sauté for 3 minutes. Then add potato, salt, pepper and red pepper and bake for 10 minutes at 400°. Serve hot with chopped parsley. Great side dish for lamb.

Purée di Patate

Creamy Mashed Potatoes

Serves 8

3 lbs. idaho potatoes
3/4 stick unsalted butter,
  cut into bits and softened
1 cup heavy cream or milk,
  heated until hot
salt to taste
white pepper to taste
pinch nutmeg

1 Bring a large pot of water to a boil, enough to cover the potatoes and add salt to taste. Peel potatoes and quarter. Add potatoes to water, then return to a boil. Gently boil potatoes until tender, 15 to 20 minutes, and drain in a colander.

2 Force potatoes, while still warm, through ricer or food mill into a large bowl. Add butter and stir with a wooden spoon, letting butter melt completely. Add 1 cup cream and incorporate by gently stirring with wooden spoon, adding more cream to thin to the desired consistency. At the last minute add a pinch of nutmeg.

3 You can add to mashed potatoes many other ingredients. I like adding roasted garlic to the mashed potatoes, truffle oil, Gorgonzola or mushrooms.

Finocchi Gratinati

Gratin of Fennel

Serves 4

2 medium, fresh fennel
1/4 cup parmigiano cheese
1/4 cup butter
1/4 cup extra virgin olive oil
1/2 cup vegetable stock
  or water (see page 28)
salt and pepper to taste

1 Poach fennel in salty water for about ¹/₂ hour. Drain and cool off. Cut fennel in quarters and put aside.

2 In a baking pan, put some olive oil, layer fennel on it and add some stock. Take a little butter and put on each fennel and bake at 375° for 25 minutes.

3 If stock is too much, reduce a little more then add cheese on top and bake for 5 more minutes. Serve hot.

Basic Polenta

9 cups water
1 tbsp. salt
3 tbsp. extra virgin olive oil
3 cups cornmeal;
   coarse-grain

*If you use instant polenta it
only takes 5 minutes, follow
same recipe.*

*Approximate cooking time:
40 minutes*

1 Bring water to a boil in a large heavy pot. Add salt and
reduce heat until water is simmering.

2 Take cornmeal by the handful and add to water very
slowly, controlling the flow to a thin stream through
your fingers. To avoid lumps, stir quickly with a long han-
dled wooden spoon while adding cornmeal. If necessary,
stop adding cornmeal from time to time and beat mixture
vigorously.

3 Cook, stirring constantly, 20 to 30 minutes. Polenta
will become very thick while cooking. It is done when
it comes away cleanly from the sides of the pot.

4 Pour polenta into a large wooden board or a large platter. With a plastic spatula smooth out polenta evenly,
about 2 inches thick. Let cool 5 minutes or until polenta
solidifies.

5 Cut polenta into slices 1 inch wide and 6 inches long.
Now you can bake, grill or fry the polenta. Serve hot,
covered with your favorite sauce. Makes 6 to 8 servings.

Variations:
1) *Fried Polenta (Polenta Fritta):*
Prepare polenta and let cool completely. Cut cooled
polenta into slices 2 inches wide and 6 inches long. Pour
oil about 1 inch deep in a large skillet. Heat oil until a
1-inch cube of bread turns golden almost immediately.
Dust polenta with some flour and then fry polenta slices
on both sides until light golden. Drain on paper towels.
Serve hot.

2) *Baked Polenta:*
Spray baking sheets with butter or oil and bake polenta
for 15 minutes at 400°.

Pane Agliato

Italian Garlic Bread

Italian bread
extra virgin olive oil
garlic

1 Slice Italian bread into 1 inch thick pieces. Rub on some garlic and extra virgin olive oil. Broil for 30 seconds. Or, you can chop the garlic and then bake, not broil, for 5 minutes at 400°.

Note: Broiling will burn the chopped garlic.

Patate Arrosto

Roasted Potatoes

1 For roasted potatoes, cut potatoes into small cubes and boil potatoes for 4 minutes, al dente, and drain.

2 In a sauté pan, heat some oil, add potatoes, salt and pepper and a little rosemary and bake at 400° for 10 minutes. Serve hot.

Spinaci Saltati in Padella

Sautéed Spinach

1 In a sauté pan, heat oil with some garlic. Remove from heat and add baby fresh spinach. Bring back to the fire and stir. Add salt and pepper and cook for two minutes. Serve hot.

Fagioli all'Uccelletto

Cannellini Beans with Sage and Tomato

2 cup cannellini beans, cooked
1 cup tomato sauce
  (see page 94)
2 leaves of sage
1 clove of garlic
2 oz. extra virgin olive oil
some liquid of cooked beans,
  optional

Wine suggestion:
Sangiovese (see page 126)

1 If you use dry beans, soak them overnight in a pot of cold water.

2 Put beans in a pot with cold water, bring to a boil and let simmer for one hour. When beans are cooked, add salt (if you add salt sooner beans will not cook soft). Drain beans and save some liquid.

3 In a sauté pan, heat some oil with garlic and sage. Add beans with a little liquid. Cook for a few minutes, add tomato sauce and cook for 3 more minutes. Add chopped parsley and serve hot. This side dish is great with grilled sausage, steak and fish.

(above) A farmer's market in Rome. *(below)* A fruit stand in Riccia.

Sauce

Filetto di Pomodoro

Tomato Sauce Serves 6

32 oz. can of San Marzano
  plum Italian tomatoes
3 cloves garlic, crushed
4 whole basil leaves
1 tsp. salt
1 tbsp. oregano
1/8 cup olive oil
salt to taste

1 Sweat garlic in olive oil. Add tomatoes and seasonings. Let simmer for approximately 20 minutes. This sauce can be the mother sauce of many recipes where tomato sauce is required.

Ragú di Carne

Meat Ragú

Serves 10

3 oz. pancetta
1/2 lb. ground veal
1/2 lb. ground beef
1/2 lb. pork
1 stalk celery
1 small carrot
1/2 cup dry red wine
1 small onion
2 cups water
1 cup olive oil
3 tbsp. tomato paste
32 oz. can of San Marzano
   plum Italian tomatoes
1 oz. cream
salt and pepper to taste

1 Chop pancetta, celery, carrot and onion very small. Heat oil in a saucepan, add the vegetables. Cook for few minutes, then add the ground meats, brown well, then add the wine, tomato paste and half the water.

2 Continue to cook until the liquids are reduced, then add the remaining water. Reduce again, then add the peeled and seeded tomatoes, a pinch of salt and pepper to taste. Cover saucepan and let cook over a medium heat for 1¹/₂ hours.

3 Add the cream (optional) and correct salt and pepper to taste. The sauce is ready to serve over fresh or stuffed pasta.

Salsa Puttanesca

Puttanesca Sauce

Serves 4

extra virgin olive oil
2 cloves garlic, crushed
3 oz. capers
4 anchovy fillets
3 oz. black olives (Gaeta)
5 cups San Marzano
   plum Italian tomatoes
red pepper flakes
parsley, chopped

1 In a sauté pan, add oil and garlic. Sauté until golden. Add capers, anchovies, and olives. Stir-fry for a few seconds. Add tomatoes, bring to a boil. Simmer for 15 minutes.

2 Add red pepper flakes. (salt, optional) Add cooked pasta and chopped parsley into sauce. Toss and serve.

Basic Brown Stock

Makes ¹/₂ gallon

4 pounds veal marrow bones
   sawed into 2-inch pieces
2 pounds beef marrow bones
   sawed into 2-inch pieces
8 ounces tomato paste
4 cups chopped onions
2 cups chopped carrots
2 cups chopped celery
4 cups dry red wine
1 bouquet garni
salt and pepper to taste
2 gallons of water

1 Preheat the oven to 450° F. Place the bones in a roasting pan and roast for 1 hour.

2 Remove the bones from the oven, remove excess fat.

3 In a mixing bowl, combine the onions, carrots, and celery together. Lay the vegetables over the bones, add tomato paste and return them to the oven. Roast for 30 minutes.

4 Remove from the oven and place the roasting pan on the stove. Deglaze the pan with the red wine, using a wooden spoon, scraping the bottom of the pan for browned particles.

5 Transfer everything into a large stockpot. Add the bouquet garni and season with salt. Add the water. Bring the liquid up to a boil and reduce to a simmer. Simmer the stock for 4 hours, skimming regularly. Remove the bones from the pot and strain through a China cap or tightly meshed strainer. If you like the sauce to more thick you can mix some flour with butter and add a little to the sauce or little cornstarch mixed with water.

6 This sauce can be the mother sauce of many veal, pasta and beef recipes. The sauce should be not too thick or not too loose.

L'acqua fa male e il vino fa cantare.
English translation: Water hurts and wine makes you sing.

Pesto Genovese

Pesto Sauce

10 oz. basil leaves, cleaned
   with damp cloth
4 cloves garlic
3 oz. pignoli nuts
4 oz. pecorino romano or
   parmigiano cheese, grated
1 cup extra virgin olive oil

1 In a food processor, blend basil, garlic, and pignoli nuts. After the mixture turns to a paste, add oil and cheese. Let it return to a paste. Set aside in a bowl.

2 Cook pasta. Drop the cooked pasta and a little of the cooking water into a sauté pan. Add in the pesto, mix and serve.

3 *Variation: You can add sliced boiled potato and string beans to this dish. You can use pesto sauce with many other recipes.

Salsa Carbonara

Carbonara Sauce

Serves 4

4 eggs
black pepper to taste
1/2 cup heavy cream
1/2 cup pecorino romano or
  parmigiano cheese
3 oz. pancetta, cut into strips
1/4 cup parsley, chopped
3 tbsp. extra virgin olive oil
1/4 of an onion, chopped (optional)
1/2 cup chicken stock (see page 28)
  or pasta water
1/4 cup of white wine

1 In a small bowl, beat eggs until frothy. Add heavy cream, pepper, parsley, and cheese. Mix thoroughly and set aside.

2 In a sauté pan, add oil, pancetta and onions if desired. Pancetta will release it's own fat. Set aside.

3 Boil pasta in salted water until al dente. When pasta is almost ready, reheat pancetta. Drop the pasta into the pancetta. Add the egg mixture.

4 Toss together until eggs are lightly scrambled. Add stock or water as necessary.

Salsa Peperonata con Capperi e Olive

Peperonata with Capers & Black Olives   Serves 6

1 onion, sliced
2 yellow peppers, sliced
2 red peppers, sliced
black pepper to taste
2 oz. capers
2 oz. black olives
   (Gaeta or Calamata)
3 oz. cherry tomatoes
1/4 cup extra virgin olive oil
chopped chives, optional
parsley, optional

1 Sauté onions with extra virgin olive oil. After a couple of minutes, add peppers and stir fry until soft, about 10 minutes. Add capers, black olives and cherry tomatoes. Season to taste.

2 Cook fish or meat and garnish with the peperonata, chopped chives or parsley optional.

Salsa Champagne

Champagne Vinaigrette Dressing

Serves 4

4 tbsp. champagne vinegar
1 tbsp. dijon mustard
1/2 cup canola oil
1/4 cup honey
salt and white pepper
   to taste

1 In a small bowl mix salt, pepper, vinegar, honey and mustard. Add oil until well combined. Serve this with your favorite salad.

Salsa all' Aceto Balsamico

Balsamic Dressing

Serves 4

12 tbsp. extra virgin
   olive oil
3 tbsp. balsamic vinegar
1 tbsp. dijon mustard
1 tsp. black pepper
1 tsp. salt
1 tsp. chopped garlic
1 tsp. oregano

1 In a small bowl mix salt, pepper, oregano, garlic, mustard and vinegar slowly. Add oil until well combined. Serve this with your favorite salad.

Salsa all'Aglio e Limone

Garlic Lemon Dressing

Serves 4

12 tbsp. extra virgin
  olive oil
4 tbsp. lemon juice
1 tsp. black pepper
1 tbsp. salt
1 tbsp. chopped garlic

1 In a small bowl mix salt, pepper, oregano, garlic, and lemon juice slowly. Add oil until well combined. Serve this with your favorite salad.

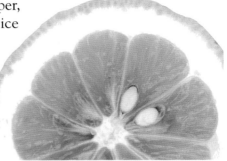

Salsa agli Agrumi

Citrus Dressing

Serves 4

12 tbsp. extra virgin olive oil
2 tbsp. lemon juice
2 tbsp. orange juice
2 tbsp. grapefruit juice
1 tbsp. salt
1 tsp. white pepper

1 In a small bowl mix salt, pepper and citrus juices until well combined.

2 Serve this with Poached Fish, Lobster, Shrimp, Tuna, Swordfish or Carpaccio.

Glassa di Marsala

Marsala Glaze

Serves 8

2 cups dry marsala
1/4 cup sugar

1 In a small sauce pot reduce marsala and sugar to $^{1}/_{4}$. Let cool and serve with meat, fish or dessert.

Glassa di Aceto Balsamico

Balsamic Glaze

Serves 8

2 cup balsamic vinegar
1/4 cup sugar

1 In a small sauce pot reduce balsamic vinegar and sugar to $^{1}/_{4}$. Let cool and serve with meat, fish or dessert.

Salsa Verde

Green Sauce

Serves 6

3 oz. fresh parsley, stems removed
1/2 oz. white bread, torn into
   pieces no crust
1 oz. capers
3 anchovy filets
2 cloves garlic
1/2 oz. red wine vinegar
1/2 cup extra virgin olive oil
salt and pepper to taste

1 Put all ingredients in a food processor or blender and mix well. Sauce should be creamy. This sauce is great with steak, poached meat or fish.

Salsa al Burro, Aceto Balsamico e Parmigiano

Butter Sauce with Balsamic Vinegar   Serves 2

4 oz. sweet butter
2 tbsp. good balsamic vinegar
2 leaves of sage
2 oz. chicken stock
(see page 28)
3 oz. Parmigiano Reggiano

1 To prepare the sauce: Melt butter into a small pan, then add the sage, balsamic vinegar and stir. You can serve this sauce with veal or fish if you like.

2 To serve with pasta, cook pasta al dente, toss in with butter sauce and sprinkled it with Parmigiano cheese. Serve quickly. If you like it more saucy, add the chicken stock.

Salsa ai Quattro Formaggi

Creamy Four-Cheese Sauce   Serves 4

8 oz. heavy cream
2 oz. parmigiano, grated
3 oz. gorgonzola or blue
cheese, cut in small pieces
3 oz. fontina cheese, diced
2 oz. mascarpone cheese
1 tsp. white pepper

1 In a sauce pot add heavy cream and all cheese. Simmer until all cheeses are blended together. Sauce should be creamy.

2 You can use this sauce with pasta, risotto or soft and fried polenta (see page 89).

Una mela al giorno leva il medico di torno.
English translation: An apple a day keeps the doctor away.

Salsa Alfredo

Alfredo Sauce

Serves 2

2 cups heavy cream
2 oz. butter
1/4 cup Parmigiano Reggiano
good amount of black pepper
  to your taste
1/2 cup hot water from the pasta

1 In a sauté pan bring to a boil heavy cream and butter. Reduce sauce to half. Add black pepper and parmigiano cheese.

2 If you use pasta, don't put cheese inside the sauce, wait until pasta is cooked. Drain pasta, toss pasta inside the sauce, then add parmigiano cheese and a little water from the pasta. This way the sauce will stick better to the pasta. Serve hot.

3 You can use this sauce as a dip dish with bread, over chicken, veal or polenta (see page 89).

Salsa al Limone

Lemon Sauce or Piccata Sauce

Serves 2

1/2 dry white wine
1 squeezed lemon
2 oz. butter
salt and pepper to taste

1 Reduce white wine to half in a sauté pan. Add lemon juice and butter. Set aside.

2 If you use this recipe for veal, chicken or shrimp, sauté meat dusted with a little flour in oil. When meat is almost cooked, add the liquid above to the pan. Cook for another minute. Sauce should be creamy. Sprinkle with chopped parsley and serve meat with wedges of lemon. You can add capers to the sauce at the very end if you desire.

Salsa Pizzaiola

Pizzaiola Sauce

Serves 2

2 cups tomato sauce (see page 94)
  or 2 cups of fresh chopped
  tomatoes
2 cloves of garlic, sliced
1/8 cup extra virgin olive oil
1 tbsp. oregano

1 In a sauce pot, heat olive oil with garlic until brown. Add tomatoes and oregano, if using fresh tomatoes add salt and pepper to taste.

2 Cook for 2-3 minutes and sauce is done. In Italy, this is the pizzaiola sauce. In the U.S.A. many people add mushrooms, peppers, onions. If you want to do that, sauté vegetables together with garlic. When vegetables are cooked, follow step one. This recipe can be used with grilled or sautéed meat or fish.

Dessert

Tiramisú

Espresso Cake with Mascarpone

1 lb. mascarpone cheese
  or cream cheese, plain
4 egg yolks
1 cup marsala wine,
  or any sweet wine
4 tbsp. sugar
10 oz. ladyfingers,
  or spongecake
3 cups espresso, or very
  strong black coffee
cocoa to decorate

1 Mix sugar, marsala and eggs in copper bowl or double boiler and cook for 5 minutes. Let cool. This mixture is called zabaglione (see page 114).

2 Blend the mascarpone cheese with the zabaglione until smooth.

3 Spread $1/3$ of the cream mixture in the bottom of a square pan 2" deep. Dip the ladyfingers individually in espresso and place uniformly on top of cream mixture. Add another $1/3$ of cream mixture and repeat another layer of ladyfingers. Add the last of the cream and refrigerate for 3 hours. Cut into squares and sprinkle with cocoa powder.

Torta di Ricotta

Italian Cheesecake

Serves 6

6 eggs
1 cup sugar
3/4 cup sweet butter
24 oz. ricotta cheese
8 oz. mascarpone cheese
1/2 oz. lemon zest
1 tsp. vanilla extract
1 tsp. orange extract
6 oz. crushed graham
  cracker crumbs

1 In a bowl mix ricotta, mascarpone, sugar and eggs until very smooth. You can use electric mixer on slow speed.

2 Add $^3/_4$ cup melted butter, lemon zest, vanilla and orange extract.

3 In a 6 or 8 inch spring form, brush with the rest of the butter and sprinkle with crushed graham cracker crumbs.

4 Add ricotta mix, sprinkle more graham cracker crumbs on top and bake for 60 minutes at 350°.

Panna Cotta con Marmellata di Frutti di Bosco

Vanilla Custard with Wild Berry Sauce

Serves 4

1/2 quart of heavy cream
1/2 cup sugar
1 vanilla stick
3 sheets of fish gelatin or
 plain gelatin powder

For sauce:
1/2 lb. mixed berries
1/2 lemon
1/4 cup sugar

1 Boil heavy cream with sugar and vanilla. Soak gelatin in cold water until soft. If using gelatin powder, follow instructions on package. Add to cream, mix and let rest for 2 hours. Put cream in 4 glasses and refrigerate for 6 hours.

2 You can put cream into a small individual aluminum ramekin (3" x 2") and let cream chill. When ready to serve, dip bottom of ramekin quickly in hot water, then flip upside down into serving plate. Decorate with fresh fruit and sauce (see below).
Option: Instead of serving on a plate, pour into a glass and top with fresh fruit and sauce.

3 For the Sauce: Put sugar, lemon juice and berries in a sauce pot and cook for a few minutes. Strain into a fine colander. Let it cool. Now you have a puree of sauce to serve with pudding.

Open Face Napoleon   Serves 6

Pastry Cream:
16 oz. milk
2 oz. sugar
2 egg yolks
1 egg
1 1/2 oz. flour
1 oz. butter
8 oz. heavy cream
vanilla extract to taste
   (can use any flavor)

1 Purchase puff pastry. Bake according to instructions, sprinkling with sugar for flavor and color.

2 Boil milk and sugar. Combine yolks, eggs and flour together. Add a little milk into the egg mixture to temper the eggs. After 4 to5 seconds add rest of the milk. Put mixture into double boiler and stir with wooden spatula until it sticks to the spatula.

3 Cook the cream and pass it through a fine colander into a glass bowl. Sprinkle with sugar on top so you will not create a film and let cool.

4 In a bowl, whip some heavy cream. Add pastry cream and gently fold together.

5 To assemble the desserts, put cream on the bottom of plate and top with crushed puff pastry (Step 1). Repeat steps one more time and then add puff pastry at the end. Garnish with fruit, powdered sugar and mint.

Torta di Cioccolato

Flourless Chocolate Cake   Serves 12

12 oz. semi-sweet chocolate
12 oz. sweet butter
12 egg yolks
12 egg whites
12 oz. sugar

Crème Anglaise:
  8 egg yolks
  4 cups heavy cream
  1 cup sugar
  vanilla extract to taste

1 Cake: Melt butter and chocolate in double boiler. Remove from heat. Beat yolks with 6 oz. sugar until smooth. Whip egg whites with 6 oz. sugar until stiff peaks form. Temper chocolate mixture with egg yolks. Slowly fold beaten egg whites into chocolate mixture.

2 Butter and sprinkle granulated sugar in 12" spring form pan & add cake mixture. Bake at 350° for 1 hour. Cool, remove from pan.

3 Créme Anglaise: Beat sugar & eggs until smooth. Add heavy cream & vanilla to saucepan. Bring to boil. Remove from heat. Temper cream mixture with egg mixture. Finish cooking in double boiler. When mixture coats the back of a wooden spoon, remove from heat. Cool in ice bath. Pour over cake.

Mousse di Cioccolato Bianco

White Chocolate Mousse

Serves 6

9 oz. white chocolate, chopped
1/2 cup + 2 tbsp. heavy cream
1 1/4 cups heavy cream
3 oz. cream of white cream de
   cacao liquor

1 Bring $1/2$ cup + 2 tbsp. heavy cream to a boil and add to chopped white chocolate. Whisk until combined. Add liquor. Cool completely.

2 Whip $1^1/_4$ cups heavy cream until soft peaks form. Gently fold into cold chocolate mixture.

3 Put chocolate mixture into a glass, let it refrigerate for 2 hours, garnish with berries or a sprig of mint.

Crema Bruciata

Crème Brûlé

Serves 6

3 cups whipping cream
5 egg yolks
1/3 cup sugar
1/3 cup packed brown sugar
1 tsp. vanilla

1 Early in the day or day ahead: In 1 quart saucepan over medium heat, heat cream until tiny bubbles form around edge of pan.

2 Meanwhile, in a 2 quart saucepan, with wire whisk, beat egg yolks with sugar until blended. Slowly stir in cream. Cook over medium, low heat, stirring constantly, until mixture just coats back of spoon, about 15 minutes (do not boil).

3 Stir in vanilla, pour into 1½ quart broiler safe casserole, refrigerate until mixture is well chilled, about 6 hours.

4 Preheat broiler. Sift brown sugar over top of chilled cream mixture. Broil 1 minute until sugar melts, making a shiny crust, chill. You can use crème brulee torch instead of broiling.

Fragole all'Aceto Balsamico

Strawberries & Balsamic Vinegar   Serves 6

1 lb. fresh strawberries washed,
   hulled or unhulled and dried
1/2 cup good-quality
   balsamic vinegar
1/2 cup sugar

1 Place strawberries in a bowl, add sugar and balsamic vinegar. Let them marinate for ten minutes, serve it with whip cream, vanilla ice cream or plain.

2 If strawberries are off season, add a little sugar to the fruit half an hour before you add vinegar.

Granita al Limone e al Caffé

Lemon Ice and Coffee Ice   Serves 4

Lemon Ice:
2 cups lemon juice
1 cup water
4 tbsp. sugar

Coffee Ice:
2 cups espresso coffee, brewed
1 cup water
4 tbsp. sugar

1 Blend all ingredients, making sure that the sugar is completely dissolved. Put the syrup into a rectangular pan and place in freezer. Every half-hour scrape the ice while freezing. It might take 3 hours to be ready. Ice should be crystallized when ready. If ice becomes too solid churn it before serving.

2 For the coffee Granita do the same thing as the lemon just replace the lemon with 2 cups of Espresso coffee.

3 You can serve the lemon ice into a nice glass with fresh, sliced lemon around it and the coffee Granita with whipped cream on top.

Al contadino non far sapere quanto è buono il formaggio con le pere.
English translation: Don't let the farmer know how good cheese is with pears.

Zabaglione Caldo con Fragole

Hot Zabaglione with Strawberries   Serves 2

2 egg yolks
4 tbsp. sugar
1/2 cup white wine
1/2 cup marsala wine
fresh strawberries

1 Whisk all ingredients, except strawberries, in double boiler over medium/high heat until you have a smooth consistency.

2 Wash, hull and slice strawberries (or any other berry) and place in goblet.

3 Spoon hot zabaglione over strawberries.

4 Variation: You can make cold Zabaglione by letting the hot Zabaglione cool off, then whip some heavy cream and fold the Zabaglione into the cream and now you will have cold Zabaglione.

Pere al Forno con Vino Rosso

Poached Pear with Red Wine

Serves 6

6 bosc pears
1 cup of sugar
3 cups dry red wine

1 Cut $1/4$ of an inch off the bottom of the pears so they are level. Put pears in a baking pan, add sugar and wine.

2 Bake at 300° for 90 minutes. Every 20 minutes make sure to wet the pear with the wine in the pan.

3 After 90 minutes the pears should be firm, but tender and the wine syrupy. Serve the pears lukewarm with the wine syrup. Add vanilla ice cream for a good combination.

L'ARTE DELLA GASTRONOMIA ITALIANA

Marcello's philosophy of wine enjoyment

I don't think there are any set rules on how to enjoy wine. One can drink (white wine with fish or red wine with red meat) because everyone has a different palate. It is more a matter of taste and instinct.

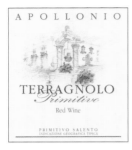

If you are at an early stage of discovering wines, trying everything is the only way to build your sensory memory and discover your own tastes. One can never make any progress with wine if you stick to the same; no matter how much you like them!

You also should work your way up going from light-bodied, medium-bodied, to full-bodied structured wines, in order to gradually educate yourself and your palate. For example, light wines like young Chiantis, mainly made of Sangiovese, or Merlot, Gamay grapes for the red wines and Riesling, Pinot Grigio, Sauvignon Blanc for the whites. Also, you don't have to break your piggy bank to enjoy a nice good wine. Save your money for later! The way I enjoy a red wine would be at a cool temperature (62°F - 65°F) and (45°F – 55°F) for a white wine, but not chilled! The choice of the glass is important. It should be a wide clear glass and have a bubble like shape in order to let your wine go around the side to observe its color, thickness and permit your wine to open itself to your sense of smell, "the bouquet".

To better enjoy your nectar, wine aficionados will tell you to open your bottle of wine one hour per year, prior consumption. Personally, I think a couple of hours will do the trick to let your wine open up (breath).

Sip your wine, don't just drink it! What I am saying is very easy: try to identify the hidden flavors inside your wine, like chocolaty, wood, berries and flower tastes.

Keep in mind, a bottle of wine comes in multiple sizes, color, or shapes, so is the content, so are people and their palate! If, at a moment or another, you are not attracted by the taste of a wine, give it another try, then if you still don't like it, it may not be for you.

A wine should be tasted with food like cheese, crackers or fruits, which have a "neutral" acidity. You might not be able to appreciate a wine to its true quality, if you have being drinking strong alcohol or vinegary food five minutes prior tasting. These will alter your palate.

Now, you are ready to ride on the multiple highways of the wine countries!

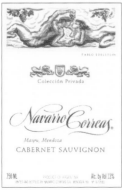

Wines of Italy

Italy is the world's largest wine producer with its wine diversity, ranging from its northern cool-temperature vineyards in the foothills of the Alps to the hot south-land. Italy has been making wine for at least 3000 years in a variety of styles, ways and from many grape varieties not widely grown outside of Italy.

The Italian varieties used for red and rosé wines include Nebbiolo, Barbera, Bonarda, Dolcetto, Lagrein, Refosco, Teroldego, Sangiovese, Aglianico, Montepulciano, Nero D'Avola and many more; for the white wines are: Pinot Grigio Pinot Bianco Cortese, Greco, Moscato, Picolit, Prosecco, Tocai, Trebbiano, Verdicchio, Vernaccia di San Gimignano, Orvieto and many more.

Other European (primarily French and German) varieties grown here are Cabernet Franc, Cabernet Sauvignon, Merlot, Pinot Nero, Syrah, Chardonnay, Pinot Bianc, Pinot Gris, Riesling Italico, and Sauvignon blanc. Some Italian wines are labeled DOC that means Denominazione di Origine Controllata ("Controlled Denomination of Origin"). The DOC wines are controlled with regard to the geographic area of production for each wine, the varieties that can be used, the minimum alcohol content, the maximum yield and specifications for aging. In 1990 tasting commissions introduced standards for appearance, color, bouquet and flavor. In addition, chemical analysis is performed to determine alcohol levels, acidity and residual sugar content. As with the systems implemented in France, Spain and other countries, the DOC system does not guarantee quality, but it does nudge a majority of the wines in that direction.

There are now over 250 DOC zones, including a small group belonging to a new, more elite level called DOCG that is Denominazione di Origine Controllata e Garantita, a category that embodies a premier group of growing areas in Italy whose regulations encompass all laws of the Denominazione di Origine Controllata are even more demanding. Meaning "Controlled and Guaranteed Denomination of Origin," the

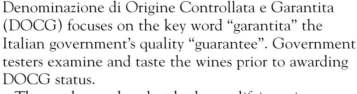

Denominazione di Origine Controllata e Garantita (DOCG) focuses on the key word "garantita" the Italian government's quality "guarantee". Government testers examine and taste the wines prior to awarding DOCG status.

The producers then bottle the qualifying wines, securing them with a government seal (a colored strip placed over the capsule or cork). The words "Denominazione di Origine Controllata e Garantita" are incorporated into the label.

The first five DOCG were Barolo and Barbaresco in the Piedmont region and Brunello Di Montalcino, Vino Nobile Di Montepulciano and Chianti in the Tuscany region. These five areas all received general approval; DOCG recent DOCG additions include Taurasi Reserve in Campania, Vernaccia Di San Gimignano in Tuscany, Asti Spumante, Moscato D'asti and Gattinara in Piedmont, Torgiano and Sagrantino Di Montefalco in Umbria. Many more techniques and grape (are) soon to be approved varieties. They haven't adapted to the many new techniques or the successful production of wines from non-traditional varieties. As a result, many excellent wines that are being produced by these modern methods or using non-traditional grapes can't qualify for DOC status. Instead, they must use the lower-ranking "Vino da tavola" classification on their labels.

Which varietals grapes are considered light and which are considered full-bodied?

The following white wines/rosés are listed from lightest to fullest-bodied: White Zinfandel, Riesling, Pinot Grigio/Pinot Gris, Sauvignon Blanc/Fumé Blanc, Pinot Blanc, Gewurztraminer, Sémillon, Viognier, Chardonnay.

The following red wines are listed from lightest to fullest-bodied: Gamay, Pinot Noir, Sangiovese, Cabernet Franc, Merlot, Syrah/Shiraz, Nebbiolo, Zinfandel, Aglianico, Cabernet Sauvignon.

Meet a part of the numerous grapes varietals from around the world:

Red Italian varietals

BAROLO DOCG (PIEDMONT)
The Barolo DOCG area lies just southwest of Alba and includes the vineyards on the steep hills around the towns of Barolo, Castiglione Falletto, Serralunga d'Alba, Monforte d'Alba and La Morra. It is one of the small number of DOCG areas in Italy, sharing this status in northwestern Italy's Piedmont region with Barbaresco, Asti Spumante and Gattinara. Like the Barbaresco DOCG, the grape used here is the Nebbiolo.

Photo by Anna Pakula

DOCG rules require Barolo wines to age for a minimum of 3 years, two of which must be in wooden barrels. "Riserva" wines require 4 years; "Riserva Speciale" wines must have 5 years. Young Barolos, which are tough, Tannin and need 5-plus years to soften, are somewhat of an acquired taste. Once they soften and open up, however, they are rich, full-bodied and can have an earthy, truffle and chocolaty characteristics with an aroma reminiscent of violets.

Marcello's recommendation:

PIO CESARE BAROLO
Produced from 100% Nebbiolo grapes. Aged in oak longer than is required by the D.O.C.G., the wine is full bodied with extraordinary finesse on the palate and a potential for great longevity. An Intense, glossy garnet red in color with faint orange reflections. Elegant scents of withered violets, blackberry jam, and faint hues of liquorice and clove. Dry and austere, slightly tannic with a background of roasted almonds.

VIETTI BAROLO
The wines of Vietti continue to defy easy characterization. The current fashion is to drop Barolo and Barbaresco producers into one of two slots: modern or traditional, but the wines of Vietti are neither modern nor traditional - they are Luca Currado in style. The wines of Vietti are the perfect example of how winemaking has evolved in Piemonte and each wine in the Vietti portfolio is an excellent wine worthy of your attention.

Others:

Gigi Rosso Barolo "Arione"	Prunotto Barolo "Bussia"	Castello di Neive Barolo
Elvio Cogno Barolo "Ravera"	Alfredo Prunotto Barolo "Bussia"	Barolo é Contrabbasso Bava
Pio Cesare Barolo	Vietti Barolo "Castiglione"	Marchesi di Barolo
Batasiolo Barolo	Gaja Barolo Sperss	
Fontanafredda Barolo La Rosa	Aurelio Settimo Rocche Barolo	

BARBARESCO DOCG (PIEDMONT)

One of the small numbers of DOCG areas in Italy, Barbaresco shares this status in northwestern Italy's Piedmont. The DOCG zone encompasses the villages of Barbaresco, Tresio and Neive, just east of Alba. The wines, which are made from the Nebbiolo grape, must be aged for 2 years, one of which is in wooden barrels. A Riserva must be aged for 3 years, one of those in wood. Considered some of Italy's best, these wines have rich, spicy flavors, and, although dry, they have a perfumed sweetness. Barbaresco wines are often

Photo by Anna Pakula

compared to Barolo wines because they are both made from Nebbiolo grapes. In the comparison, Barbaresco wines are usually regarded as more elegant and refined; the Barolos are thought to be more robust and longer-lived.

Photo by Anna Pakula

Marcello's recommendation:
Barichi Barbaresco
Angelo Gaja Barbaresco
Paitin Vanotu' Pelissero Barbaresco
Batasiolo Barbaresco
Produttori del Barbaresco
Sorì Paitin Vecchie Vigne Barbaresco
Punset "Compo Quadro" Barbaresco
Ceretto Barbaresco" Asiji

GATTINARA DOCG (PIEDMONT)

Small, recently upgraded DOCG zone located in the Piedmont region in northwestern Italy, northeast of Turin and northwest of Milan. It's one of the few DOCG areas in Italy and shares this status in the Piedmont region with Barbaresco and Barolo. The red wine is made from at least 90% Spanna (Nebbiolo) and the rest Bonarda; it requires 4 years of aging, two of which must be in wooden barrels. The wines of Gattinara had an excellent reputation from ancient times. At their best, Gattinara wines can be full-bodied and elegant with hints of violets and spice. Some are also long-lived and capable of aging for 10 to 15 years or more.

Marcello's recommendation:
Travaglini Gattinara
Gaja Gattinara
Nervi Gattinara

Photo by Anna Pakula

BARBERA (PIEDMONT)

Italian red wine grape that can produce marvelous wines but that has become so plentiful in some of the hotter growing regions around the world that its image is beginning to tarnish. Barbera wines from these hotter areas-such as southern Italy and California's San Joaquin Valley, are high in alcohol and acid. They have little flavor and are used mainly as blending wine. Superior Barbera wines can exhibit a ripe currant flavor with a nuance of smokiness. Five DOCs in Italy's Piedmont region produce the most noteworthy Barbera wines. Two of them - Barbera D'Alba and Barbera D'asti - make wines that are 100 % Barbera, while Barbera del Monferrato, Colli Toronesi, and Rubino di Cantavenna may produce blended wines. Good Barbera wines are also made by the DOC's of Oltre Po Pavese in Lombardy and Colli Bolognesi and Colli Piacentini in Emilia (where Barbera is called Gutturnio).

Photo by Anna Pakula

Photo by Anna Pakula

Marcello's recommendation:
Baricchi Barbera d'Alba
Deep reddish purple color with fresh, young with garden scents. Full and balanced taste, with a note of almond on the finish. Perfect with appetizers, Bresaola, cheeses, flavorful risottos, poultry and white meats.
Others:
Michelle Chiarlo Barbera d'Asti
Coppo Barbera d'Asti "Camp du Rouss"
Vietti Barbera d'Asti
Giocomo Bologna Bricco Barbera
Bava Barbera d'Asti Stradivario
Deltetto Barbera d'Alba Rocca delle Marasche

LAGREIN (ALTO ADIGE)

The lagrein grape is unique to the Alto Adige, and its flavor is, unlike any other, black fruit flavors, along with a savory, tarry, almost meaty edge that is a trademark of Lagrein.

Marcello's recommendation:
Muri Gries Alto Adige Lagrein
Dunkel Muri
Abbazia di Novacella Lagrein
100% Lagrein grape

Photo by Anna Pakula

Photo by Anna Pakula

DOLCETTO (PIEDMONT)

Red wine grape, whose name translates to "little sweet one," that is grown mainly in the southwest section of Italy's Piedmont region. There are several theories for Dolcetto's name. One suggests that it is because of the sweetness of the grapes and the juice they produce. Another one says it is because there is a perception of sweetness in Dolcetto wines, even though they are usually vinified as dry wines without residual sugar Dolcetto wines have high acidity and are usually deep purple in color. They have perfumy Bouquet and rich, fruity, ripe-berry flavors, sometimes with a slightly bitter aftertaste. They should be drunk young before the fruit starts to fade. There are seven DOCs for Dolcetto, all in the Piedmont region. They are Dolcetto d'Aqui, Dolcetto d'Asti, Dolcetto di Diano d'Alba, Dolcetto delle Langhe Monregalesi, Dolcetto di Dogliani, Dolcetto di Ovada, the best known is Dolcetto D'Alba.

Marcello's recommendation:
Villadoria Dolcetto d'Alba
Ruby red color with violet reflections. Fresh and youthful bouquet with garden scents. Full and balanced with a note of almond on the finish. Perfect with appetizers, cheeses, mushrooms, salmon, tuna or swordfish, white meat and poultry. Serve very slightly chilled (about 15 minutes in the refrigerator).

Others:
Prunotto Dolcetto d'Alba
Pio Cesare Dolcetto d'Alba
Giacosa Dolcetto d'Alba
Punset Compo Re

Photo by Anna Pakula

Photo by Anna Pakula

TEROLDEGO ROTALIANO (TRENTINO)

Here's an unusual entry worth recording if you're keeping a "life list" of grape varieties tasted. Teroldego Rotaliano is grown in Trentino, in northeastern Italy. This wine shows inky dark reddish-purple. Deep black-fruit aroma, prunes and plums and hints of licorice. Soft and juicy fruit flavor, tar and smoke.

Marcello's recommendation:
Foradori Teroldego Rotaliano
Zeni Teroldego Rotaliano

RECIOTO DELLA VALPOLICELLA DOC; RECIOTO DELLA VALPOLICELLA AMARONE DOC (VENETO)

These wines are made primarily from the red Corvina grape, but also with Rondinella, Molina, and others. They are not like other Valpolicella wines because of the special process that Recciotto wines go through, such as the use of semi-dried grapes. The Recioto della Valpolicella, with its cherry and plum flavors, can be sweet and quite pleasant. The Recioto della Valpolicella Amarone (also called Amarone della Valpolicella) is the Dry version, which is essentially the same as the sweet except that it's allowed to Ferment fully. It too can be quite good, with similar flavors, but a bittersweet essence. Amarone wines are unique in the Valpolicella region made from 70% of Corvina, 20% Rondinella & 10% Molinara grapes.

Photo by Anna Pakula

Marcello's recommendation:
Allegrini Palazzo della Torre

This blend of Corvina (70%), Rondinella (25%) and Sangiovese (5%) is a smooth, full-bodied cru made in an innovative ripasso style, which is a process where the finished wine is "passed back over" the skins used to produce Amarone or Recioto, causing a second fermentation to take place. In this unique case, 70% of the grapes picked are vinified immediately. The remaining 30% are left to dry until the end of December when they are vinified and re-fermented with the wine from the fresh grapes. The result is higher alcohol content, rounder style, lower acidity and more extraction than a Valpolicella.

Photo by Anna Pakula

Others:
Tommasi Amarone
Cesari Amarone
Bertani Amarone
   "Recioto Valpolicella"
Allegrini Valpolicella Classico
Allegrini Amarone
Villa Spinosa-Amarone
Speri Amarone
Romano Dal Forno Amarone

SANGIOVESE (TUSCANY)

Etymologists believe this red grape's name is derived from sanguis Jovis meaning "the blood of Jove (Jupiter)". Its beginnings are thought to pre-date Roman times. Sangiovese is one of the top two red grapes (the other being Nebbiolo) in Italy, where it is extensively planted, particularly in the central and southern regions. It is believed to originate in Tuscany, where it dominates today. Sangiovese wines are high in acid, with moderate to high tannins and medium levels of alcohol. The flavors have a hint of earthiness and are usually not boldly fruity. Sangiovese wines are not deeply colored and often have a slightly orange tint around the edges. Most are not long-lived and will last for less than 10 years. Of the numerous strains of this grape, Sangiovese Grosso and Sangiovese Piccolo have taken the lead. Compared to Sangiovese Piccolo's smaller grape clusters, Sangiovese Grosso has larger, more loosely bunched grapes. It is also more widely cultivated and yields a larger crop.

One strain of Sangiovese Grosso is Brunello ("little dark one"), so named for the brown hue of its skin. It is the grape responsible for the potent and long-lived Brunello Di Montalcino wines, which are made totally from this variety. Prugnolo is Montepulciano's local name for the Sangiovese Grosso grape, which produces the Vino Nobile Di Montepulciano wines. Though Sangiovese is the dominant grape in Italy's well-known Chianti wines, it must officially (for DOC qualification) be blended with other varieties, including a percentage of white grapes. Fortunately, the maximum allowable Sangiovese (also known as Sangioveto in Chianti) went from 80 to 90% percent in 1984, which allows Chianti wines to have a more robust character. Some producers, particularly in Tuscany, are now making non-DOC wines either using only Sangiovese grapes or blending them with small amounts of Cabernet Sauvignon. Cabernet is a particularly complimentary partner that lends bouquet, structure. Outside Italy, small amount of Sangiovese can be found in California.

Marcello's recommendation:
Rocca Delle Macie Ser Gioveto
100% Sangiovese, Bright ruby red, intense, mature fruit aromas, rich, well structured, berry fruit flavors.

Others:
Badia a Coltibuono "Rosso Cancelli"
 100% Sangiovese
Checchi Spargolo, *100% Sangiovese*
Crognolo Sette Ponti, *90% Sangiovese*

Photo by Anna Pakula

CHIANTI DOCG (TUSCANY)

Well-known wine-producing area located in Tuscany in central Italy. Located in the Tuscany region. The Chianti DOCG is a single appellation, but is divided into seven sub zones, the most famous being Chianti Classico, which runs from the Florence area south to the Siena region.

The remaining six sub zones are: Chianti Aretini, Chianti Colli Fiorentini, Chianti Colli Senesi, Chianti Colline Pisane, Chianti Montalbano, and Chianti Rufina. The wines from Chianti Classico, which are usually identifiable by a black rooster (gallo nero) on the label, are generally more well known and of better quality than those from the other six areas. But within the Chianti area, it may only be labeled "Chianti."

Chianti wines are made from four grape varieties - with at least 75% Sangiovese and the rest blend of Canaiolo, Trebbiano, and Malvasia. Today, however, Cabernet Sauvignon is being added to some Chianti blends. The word "Riserva" on the label indicates that the wine is of superior quality and has been aged for at least 3 years before being released.

Marcello's recommendation:
Castello di Bossi "Berardo" Chianti Classico Riserva
A rich, luminous ruby red. Appealing, crisp notes of menthol emerge on the nose, blending beautifully with more developed aromas reminiscent of cinchona and tamarind. The wine enters smooth and almost creamy, massive and full, but not in the least aggressive. Tannins are well integrated with the alcohol, and a seductive, tasty finish lingers quite long.

COLI CHIANTI RISERVA
80% Sangiovese with Canaiolo, Trebbiano and Malvasia del Chianti. Dark ruby-red color. Rich, spicy, black-berry bouquet. Luscious cherry and vanilla flavors leading to a long, smooth finish.

Photo by Anna Pakula

RUFFINO "DUCALE GOLD" CHIANTI CLASSICO RISERVA

Bright appearance, dark color, a very nice dark fruit nose with good intensity,
some raspberry on palate, nicely concentrated with optimal balance and length.

ROCCA DELLE MACIE CHIANTI CLASSICO

Lively ruby red. Nose: intense and persistent with hints of wild berries that combine
well with the aromas released by the wood of the barrels. Palate: savory and full bodied,
it highlights the exceptional persistence of the bouquet.

Others:

Ruffino"Il Leo" Chianti Superiore

Melini Laborel Chianti Classico Riserva

Palladio Chianti

Dievole Chianti Classico

Rocca delle Macie Chianti Classico

Castellare Chianti Classico

Castello di Bossi Chianti Classico

Nozzole Giovanni Folonari Chianti Classico

VINO NOBILE DI MONTEPULCIANO DOCG (TUSCANY)

Vino Nobile di Montepulciano wines are made from 60 to 80% Prugnolo (Sangiovese), 10 to 20%
Canaiolo and up to 20% of other varieties (although no more than 10% white). One of the other
red varieties most often used is the Mammolo, which adds the scent of violets to the bouquet.
White grapes like Trebbiano and Malvasia are no longer required, which allows winemakers to
produce wines that are more intense and longer-lived. The wines of this DOCG must be aged for
2 years in oak or chestnut casks, 3 years for those labeled Riserva.

Marcello's recommendations:

Fattoria del Cerro Vino Nobile di Montepulciano

Avignonesi Vino Nobile di Montepulciano

Santa Venere Vino Nobile di Montepulciano

Photo by Anna Pakula

Photo by Anna Pakula

Photo by Anna Pakula

BRUNELLO DI MONTALCINO DOCG (TUSCANY)

The wines from Brunello di Montalcino are regarded as some of Italy's best. They are made totally from Sangiovese Grosso called Brunello di Montalcino. The wines are big, deep-colored, and powerful, with enough tannins and structure to be quite long-lived. Brunello di Montalcino wines have one of the longest aging requirements in Italy - 4 years, 3 of which must be in wooden barrels. The Riserva must age for 5 years. This DOCG zone encompasses the vineyards around the hillside town of Montalcino, which is south and slightly east of Siena in the southern portion of Tuscany.

Marcello's recommendation:
Castello Banfi Brunello di Montalcino

Brunello is perhaps the most respected red of Italy. Aged for a total of up to four years, including a minimum of two years in oak barrels. This wine is a wine of robust character. It possesses a rich garnet color, and a depth, complexity and opulence that is softened by an elegant, lingering aftertaste. Castello Banfi Brunello di Montalcino's regal qualities are best exhibited with game, red meats, roasts, hearty stews and rich powerful cheeses such as Parmigiano Reggiano.

Others:
Campogiovanni Brunello di Montalcino
Castello Banfi Poggio All'Oro Brunello
Angelo Sasseti Brunello di Montalcino
Il Poggione Brunello di Montalcino Riserva
Biondi Santi Brunello di Montalcino
Rosso di Montalcino Ranieri

Photo by Anna Pakula

SUPER-TUSCANS VINI DA TAVOLA

Are produced using alternate methods (like aging in small, nontraditional oak barrels), alternate varieties (like Cabernet Sauvignon, Merlot, Syrah) or an alternate composition (like using 100 percent Sangiovese, made in areas where it is not approved). Although placed in the Vini Da Tavola category, these super-Tuscans are in some cases superior to DOCG wines and are able to command higher prices.

Marcello's recommendation:
Villa Banfi Col di Sasso
which translates to "Stony Hill," is a blend of Cabernet Sauvignon and Sangiovese grapes cultivated on the most rocky and impervious slopes of the Banfi estate in Montalcino, Tuscany. Typically harvested in early October, each grape variety is vinified separately. The Sangiovese imparts body, while stainless steel aged Cabernet Sauvignon adds fruit and structure.
Biondi Santi Sassoalloro
90% Sangiovese Grosso, 10% Cabernet Sauvignon
Shows bright blackberry, with hints of plum on the nose. Full-bodied, with silky tannins and lots of lively acidity. Needs bottle age to come together.
Carpineto Dogajolo
Sangiovese and Cabernet Sauvignon
Very fruity and intense, typical of a young wine, with pronounced overtones of wood typically found   in aged wines. Full, soft on the palate and well-developed. A very easy drinking wine.

Photo by Anna Pakula

Photo by Anna Pakula

QUERCIAVALLE ARMONIA
This wine is obtained from a scrupulous and particular selection of the Tuscan Sangiovese and Canaiolo grapes which are products of the select 40 year old vines on the Losi-Querciavalle Estate. The percentages of grape that this wine is composed of are 90 - 95% Tuscan Sangiovese and 5 - 10% Tuscan Canaiolo. Aged first in French Barrique and then in small Slavonic Oak barrels. After the wood maturation, the wine is then bottled and left for a brief period to rest in the bottle for further refinement. The actual periods of maturation in both the barrique and the bottles is difficult to say because it varies with each production, since the characteristics of the grapes are so diverse. The color is an intense ruby red with granite reflections. The aroma is intense with a hint of vanilla and spice, a full, smooth flavor and elegant structure.

ANTINORI SANTA CRISTINA

This well made red is the ideal choice for those look-ing for a nice medium bodied wine. Already recog-nized as one of the "World's Greatest Wine Values" by Robert Parker, the Santa Cristina is comprised of 90% Sangiovese and 10% Merlot. You'll love the cherry-strawberry bouquet and ripe, straightforward red berry flavors on the palate. A beauty of a wine from the King of Tuscan wines!

QUICCIARDINI STROZZI MILLIANI
60% Cabernet 40% Merlot

Classy and powerful wine made from a modern blend of Sangiovese, Cabernet Sauvignon, and Merlot. Aromas of black fruit, coffee, and a grassy note give way to a sumptuous and warm palate; the elegant, fine tannins in its structure allude to good longevity.

CASTELLO DI BOSSI CORBAIA
70% Sangiovese 30% Cabernet Sauvignon

A deep ruby red, with slight garnet highlights in the background. On the nose, a vein of fruit preserve melds well with more developed characteristics, such as elegant, delicate nuances of tobacco and coffee.

The attack is solid and powerful, bolstered by a decisive suite of finely-woven tannins well-integrated into the structure. Very appealing, lengthy finish. Dogajolo 80% Sangiovese & 20% Cabernet from Tuscany.

Very fruity and intense, typical of a young wine, with pronounced overtones of wood typically found in aged wines. Full, soft on the palate and well-developed. A very easy drinking wine.

Carpineto's Dogajolo is one of the most innovative wines to be found, it embodies all the characteristics that one most appreciates; youthful vigour, mature wood, smoothness and a fruity and fragrant bouquet - qualities not often found in any one wine!

Castello Di Bossi photography archive.

Castello Di Bossi photography archive.

Castello Di Bossi photography archive.

Others:

Castellare Sodi di San Niccolo
  85% Sangioveto, 15% Malvasia Nera

Fattoria Le Pupille Saffredi
  50% Cabernet Sauvignon, 35% Merlot,
  15% Alicante

Castello di Gabbiano Per Ania
  100% Sangiovese Grosso

Ornellaia Le Serre Nuove
  Sangiovese, Cabernet Sauvignon, Merlot

Bolgheri Ornellaia, *80% Cabernet Sauvignon*
  15% Merlot, 5% Cabernet Franc

Gaja Gaja Ca'Marcanda
  50% Merlot, 25% Cabernet Sauvignon,
  25% Cabernet Franc

Montalcino Villa di Corsano
  70% Sangiovese, 20% Cabernet Sauvignon,
  10% Merlot

Antinori Guado al Tasso, *Cabernet, Merlot, Syrah*

Bolgheri Sassicaia, *80% Cabernet, 10% Merlot,*
  10% Sangiovese

Argiano Solengo
  25% Cabernet, Merlot, Sangiovese & Syrah

San Felice Vigorello
  60% Sangiovese, 40% Cabernet Sauvignon

Rissecoli Saeculum
  60% Sangiovese, 30% Cabernet
  10% Merlot

Brancaia *65% Sangiovese, 35% Cabernet Sauvignon*

Antinori Solaia
  75% Cabernet, 20% Sangiovese,
  5% Cabernet Franc

Tenuta dell'Ornellaia "Le Volte"
  Sangiovese, Cabernet, Merlot Castello Banfi

Summus, *45% Sangiovese, 40% Cabernet*
  Sauvignon, 15% Syrah

Fontodi Flaccianello, *100% Sangiovese*

Barone Ricasoli Casalferro
  100% Sangiovese

Antinori Tignanello
  80% Sangiovese, 15% Cabernet,
  5% Cabernet Franc

Mondavi Frescobaldi Luce
  50% Sangiovese, 50% Merlot

Ludovico Antinori Ornellaia
  80% Cabernet, 20% Merlot

Castello Banfi Excelsus
  60% Cabernet Sauvignon, 40% Merlot

Folonari Tenute-Cabreo Il Borgo
  70% Sangiovese, 30% Cabernet Sauvignon

Photo by Anna Pakula

Castello Di Bossi photograph archive

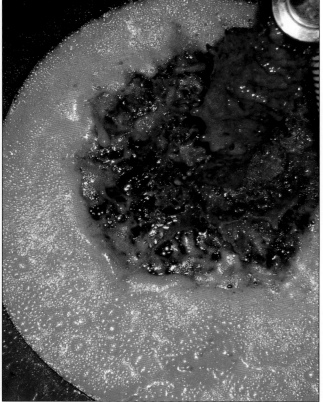

Photo by Anna Pakula

MONTEFALCO ROSSO SAGRANTINO DOC (UMBRIA)

A small hilltop town located southeast of Perugia in Italy's Umbria region. The DOC zone covers the vineyards on the slopes around Montefalco, plus those of several neighboring villages. Montefalco makes a good-quality, full-flavored Rosso out of Sangiovese, Trebbiano, and Sagrantino plus small amounts of Barbera, Ciliegiolo, Merlot, Malvasia and Montepulciano. However, it is the Sagrantino di Montefalco wines-made in both Dry and Passito versions from Sagrantino grapes that are creating this area's reputation. These wines are Rich and full-bodied with adequate tannins to let them age for a while. In recognition of its high-quality wines, the Sagrantino di Montefalco zone was upgraded to DOCG status in the mid-1990s.

Others:
Tiburzi Sagrantino di Montelfalco
Arnaldo Caprai "Collepiano"
  Sagrantino di Montelfalco
Adanti Aquarta Montefalco Rosso
Tiburzi Montefalco Rosso

Photo by Anna Pakula

Photo by Anna Pakula

Photo by Anna Pakula

Photo by Anna Pakula

MONTEPULCIANO D'ABRUZZO DOC
(ABRUZZO)

It is located in central Italy's Abruzzo region and that is not related to the Vino Nobile Di Montepulciano which is named after a town in the Tuscany region. Montepulciano D'Abruzzo is named after the grape variety Montepulciano which must make up at least 85% of this DOC wine (the rest is Sangiovese. Montepulciano D'Abruzzo DOC wines are generally ordinary, although several producers who keep Yield low the produce good, full-bodied wines capable of long aging for a minimum The same grapes go into a Cerasuolo (dry Rose), which is considered quite good.

Photo by Anna Pakula

Others:

Zaccagnini Montepulciano d'Abruzzo
A rustic wine with a distinct nose of plums, pepper and chocolate.

Illuminati Montepulciano d'Abruzzo "Riparosso"
The color is an intense ruby red with a distinct, pleasant vinous fragrance. The flavor is dry and savory with soft tannins. Riparosso is a great accompaniment with roasted or braised red meats as well as poultry and savory dishes: ideal with lamb. Tomato based pasta without a doubt a delicious red wine and one of the best buys in all the red wine categories. Serve at room temperature.

Di Maio Norante, Don Luigi from Molise
Full-blown red with loads of toasted oak and "jammy" aromas. Full-bodied, chewy with voluptuous tannin, a long berry and vanilla after taste.

Photo by Anna Pakula

Others:
Capestrano
Montepulciano
D'Abruzzo

Valentini
Montepulciano
D'Abruzzo

Mascarelli
Montepulciano
D'Abruzzo

AGLIANICO (CAMPANIA/BASILICATA)

One of the higher-quality red wine grapes found in southern Italy, mainly in Campania and Basilicata Aglianico is thought to have been planted in this region as early as the seventh century b.c. The best 100 percent Aglianico wines come from Taurasi; followed by those from Aglianico del Volture both have DOC status. The wines from these two DOCs are noted for their roughness when young due to high tannin, noticeable acidity, and a dense concentration of flavors; they're definitely built for aging. As these wines mature, they can exhibit great balance with subtle fruit flavors and earthy, tarry, and chocolaty characteristics.

Photo by Anna Pakula

Marcello's recommendation:
Re Manfredi Aglianico del Vultur
Paternoster "Don Anselmo" Aglianico
De Conciliis "Donna Luna" Aglianico
De Conciliis"Naima", *100% Aglianico*
Mastroberardino Taurasi Radici Aglianico
Struzziero Taurasi "Riserva"

NEGRO AMARO (PUGLIA)

Negro Amaro ('black bitter') is grown in the southern Salento Peninsula of Puglia , the favored grape in Salice Salentino. Negro amaro makes a dusty-tasting wine with traces of leather and earth, even the barnyard. These can dominate fruit, and it is often blended with fruity Malvasia Nera to compensate.

Marcello's recommendation:
Taurino Salice Salentino
This deep ruby purple wine is big and peppery with a spicy bouquet and rich, abundantly endowed lingering flavors.

Others:
Leone De Castris Salice Salentino
Cantele Salice Salentino

Photo by Anna Pakula

NERO D'AVOLA (SICILY)

It is Sicily's most popular red grape, used in the region's bestselling varietal wine. Until the 1980s, commercial use of Nero d'Avola was dedicated almost exclusively to fortifying weaker reds in France and northern Italy. In the past Nero d'Avola, like other Sicilian reds, was often syrupy, with an alcohol content reaching eighteen percent - too strong as table wines. The name, which literally means "Avola Black," is a good description.

New viticulture techniques and night harvesting — placing the grapes in cooled vats to present premature fermentation — have been used by a few vintners to retain flavor without producing an over powering wine. The result is often compared to Syrah, another popular red. Boasting a singular climate, Sicily is blessed with consistent growing seasons from year to year, typified by lots of warm sunshine and very little rain. Vintage quality varies, of course, but not as much as it does in Burgundy or Piedmont.

Marcello's recommendation:
Duca Enrico di Salaparuta
100% Nero D'Avola from Sicily
Duca Enrico, a 100% Nero d'Avola and the 2001 is excellent. Nero d'Avola is the most famous indigenous varietal of Sicily and its exotic tobacco and chocolate flavors only add to its appeal. Here all the flavors are seamlessly woven to create a rich, spicy red with layers of flavor and subtle spice. Above all the tannins are polished and the wine is elegant on the palate and in the finish.

Planeta Santa Cecilia
100% Nero D'Avola
Aged for 12 months in French oak barriques, 14% alcohol. Annual production 70, 000 bottles. Showing a bright, lively nose with some rich, herby complexity, this is an interesting wine. The elegant palate shows a good concentration of dense fruit, dry tannins and high acidity.

Others:
Donnafugata, Mille e una Notte
Antichi Vinai Tre Riviere Rosso Nero D'Avola

White Italian varietals

PROSECCO (VENETO/LOMBARDIA)

A white-wine grape that is grown primarily in the eastern part of Italy's Veneto region. Prosecco's made into lightly sparkling (frizzante), fully sparkling (spumante) and still wine. Its fine reputation, however, comes from the sparkling versions. The wines are crisp and appley and, though they can be sweet, are more often found dry. The best-known wines made principally from Prosecco come from the DOC of Prosecco di Conegliano-Valdobbiadene and are generally

sold with either the name of Conegliano or Valdobbiadene attached. The very best Prosecco wines are labeled "Superiore di Cartizze" and come from a sub zone within Valdobbiadene. Prosecco is also known as Balbi, Glera, Serprina, and Tondo.

Marcello's recommendation:
Mionetto Il Prosecco

A straw-colored wine with brilliant reflections. The aroma is fruity, reminiscent of pear and citrus with a slightly floral bouquet. The wine is fresh and crisp with apparent apple and peach flavors. This lightly sparkling (Frizzante) wine typifies the traditional wine-maker's Prosecco.

Others:
Zardetto Prosecco

SPUMANTE (PIEDMONT)

Italian for "sparkling," "foamy," or "frothy," referring to fully sparkling wines, as opposed to those that are slightly sparkling spumante is made throughout Italy from a variety of different grapes The most renowned of the spumante is the sweet Asti Spumante from the Piedmont region, which is made from the Muscat grape.

Martini & Rossi Asti Spumante Piedmont

Italy's most famous Spumante is a Moscato-based sweet sparkling wine delicious as an aperitif or with desserts and fruit. A wonderful and fragrant aroma of peach and pear with honey highlights.

Others:
Bruno Giacosa, Brut Spumante, Piedmont

ARNEIS (PIEDMONT)

In Piedmontese dialect, Arneis means difficult or stubborn. This is the characteristic of the varietal. Due to its very delicate skin it is a difficult grape to grow well. Most wine makers choose to rise to these challenges and enjoy this wine specifically for its difficulty. Subtle perfumes of apple, pear and peach. A very refreshing white recommended with a wide variety of foods, especially antipasti and pasta dishes.

Marcello's recommendation:
Bruno Giacosa Arneis
Molino Arneis
Malvira "Roero Arneis Saglietto"

TOCAI FRIULANO (FRIULI)

The most widely planted and most often drunk wine throughout the areas of the Friuli region. Its name is said to be derived from the local word for the small juice-style glass used to serve wine in Friulian taverns and restaurants. While there is some controversy as to whether Tocai Friulano came from Hungary or was exported to it, the grape and the wine it makes have no connection to Tokaj or to France's Tokay d'Alsace. It is believed to be the grape known as Sauvignon Vert.

Pale straw-yellow, Tocai Friulano carries an enticing nuance of wildflowers and pears. It is broadly flavored and can offer notes of herbs and citrus. Very nicely balanced acidity heightens the flavors and gives it a long, clean finish.

This Wine is great with seafood! Especially sushi, clams and grilled shrimp. Stay away from cheeses.

Marcello's recommendation:
Toh di Lenardo Tocai
Livio Feluga Tocai

Photo by Anna Pakula

PINOT GRIGIO (FRIULI/TRENTINO/VENETO)

Like Pinot Blanc, one of the white grapes of the Pinot family and like Riesling and Gewürztraminer, Pinot Grigio loves cold climates. The most renowned Pinot Grigio comes from the northernmost regions of Italy, especially those regions that border the Alps, as well as Alsace, where it is known as Pinot Gris or, confusingly, as "tokay." In the U.S., Oregon is emerging as the top state for delicious lively Pinot Gris with light almond, lemon and vanilla flavors.

Maso Canali Pinot Grigio

This wine has a brilliant golden color with a very pleasant nose marked by apricot, tropical lemon and pineapple flavors, complemented by floral and spicy notes. This elegantly balanced wine exhibits ripe fruit flavors on the palate and a lasting, enlivening finish.

Photo by Anna Pakula

Photo by Anna Pakula

Wine/Vineyards 139

Photo by Anna Pakula

Livio Feluga Pinot Grigio
A clean style makes this our choice for a summer brunch wine. The nose of tropical fruits, rose petals & tulips are almost enticing enough to dab behind the ears. Full & fresh in the mouth with great acidity, it finishes with lingering flavors of mango, apple & bananas.

Zenato Pinot Grigio
90% Pinot Grigio + a small percentage of other local varieties harvested from August 20th to September 10th. The grapes were crushed and fermented in temperature controlled, stainless steel tanks for 15-20 days. After fermentation, the wine was stabilized in tank for 4 months prior to being bottled and released to the market. Pale yellow in color with greenish highlights. A wine to be enjoyed while it is young and shows the freshest fruit. Refreshing and soft with a smooth, dry finish.

HOFSTATTER PINOT GRIGIO
One of the best pinot Grigio a well-rounded body with floral aromas and ripe fruit flavors, and well balanced in acidity. A long, smooth finish.

Others:
Pighin Pinot Grigio,
Kris Pinot Grigio
Torre Di Luna Pinot Grigio
Banfi Pinot Grigio Sant' Angelo
Santa Margherita Pinot Grigio

Photo by Anna Pakula

Photo by Anna Pakula

PINOT BIANCO (FRIULI/TRENTINO/VENETO)

One of the white grapes of the pinot family that includes Pinot Grigio (also white) and the red grapes Pinot Noir and Pinot Meunier. While some Pinot Blanc can be found interspersed with chardonnay in the vineyards of Burgundy, the grape is more renowned in Alsace. In North America, California boasts several top producers of Pinot Blanc, though the grape is not widely grown. Pinot Blanc often has flavors similar to Chardonnay, though the wine is generally lighter in body and somewhat more delicate.

Marcello's recommendation:
Masùt da Rive Pinot Bianco
This wine Straw yellow in color with green highlights. Floral and ripe apple aromas. the wine is soft and harmonious on the palate with sensations of almonds and ripe peach. The finish is smooth and pleasing. Food Pairing: Aperitif; mild cheeses, pasta dishes, fresh seafood or seafood soup.

Volpe Pasini Pinot Bianco
This Pinot Bianco has a light straw yellow color with green highlights. The aromas are delicate, almost ethereal, and will remind you of small berries and delicate flowers even roses. Very harmonious and possessing good character, this wine exhibits much elegance and finesse and the flavors are gentle and supple.this Pinot Bianco will marry well with most appetizers as well as with risotto and soups; it will also match well with poultry and fresh soft cheese. Best served at 55°F.

Others:
Alois Lageder Pinot Bianco
Puiatti Pinot Bianco

Photo by Anna Pakula

CORTESE DI GAVI (PIEDMONT)

Gavi is produced in the Alto Monferrato, a viti vini cultural zone situated in the southern part of the province of Alessandria. A total of 59 communes are involved in its output in a district that is predominantly hilly. Acqui, Ovada and Gavi are the best-known communities in its production zone. Gavi is made exclusively from Cortese grapes.

Although that variety is extremely ancient, documentary evidence of its existence goes back only several centuries. The first fairly detailed account of the Cortese variety is provided by the ampelography of Piedmontese grapes compiled by Count Nuvolone, deputy director of the Agrarian Society of Turin, in 1798. The Count wrote that the Cortese variety "has rather elongated clusters and somewhat large grapes. When they are ripe, they become yellow and are good to eat. They make good wine and in substantial quantity. And it keeps well."

Photo by Anna Pakula

Other sources have cited production since the end of the 19th century in various parts of the region, including "old Piedmont." And the variety has been widely praised for its purity as well as its output. Today, cultivation of Cortese, which is highly resistant, is especially intensive in the area bounded by the Bormida and Scrivia rivers in the province of Alessandria. Its grapes yield the most important of Piedmont's dry white wines, which received its Denominazione di Origine Controllata in 1974.

Marcello's recommendation:
La Scolca Gavi di Gavi "Black Label"
The most famous producer of the Cortese grape. Crisp, fragrant and full-bodied, often compared to French white Burgundy for its weight and elegance.

Principessa Gavi
A crisp, clean stainless steel fermented Gavi with balanced acidity and fresh citrus and pear flavors.

Others:
Cortese Di Gavi Pio Cesare
Gavi di Gavi Bava

Photo by Anna Pakula

Vernaccia di San Gimignano (Tuscany)

A DOCG A white-wine grape grown in Italy's Tuscany region, primarily southwest of Florence around the medieval hilltop town of San Gimignano. Vernaccia di San Gimignano dates back as far as the thirteenth century and its origins are thought to be Greek. The wines produced from this variety vary tremendously. Traditionally made, they're golden in color, rich, and full-bodied, with an oxidized style and a slightly bitter edge to the flavor. More modern winemaking techniques produce paler-colored wines with crisper, lighter characteristics.

Photo by Anna Pakula

A DOCG area based around the town of San Gimignano that was the very first to receive DOC status when Italy began implementing its wine-classification system in 1966. In addition to the reputation for the wines produced from its namesake grape, the town of San Gimignano is renowned for its medieval atmosphere. It is replete with tall, narrow towers that were built during a time when higher was considered better and safer.

Photo by Anna Pakula

Marcello's recommendation:
San Quirico Vernaccia di San Gimignano DOCG
Made from 100% Vernaccia grown in hillside vineyards surrounding the Tuscan town of San Gimignano. The grapes were harvested in September/October and were vinified in stainless steel tanks under controlled temperatures. Vernaccia holds the distinction of being the very first appellation to receive DOC status.

Teruzzi & Puthod Terre di Tuffi

A white wine offering from Tuscany has intriguing greenish brass colors and modest, but interesting, apple and spice aromas. Flavors are more pronounced, with minerally crisp green apple notes and grapefruit citrus, very crisp on the palate. The green apple lingers on the finish, picking up notes of almond blossom and nutmeg. Made from the Tuscan Vernaccia grape, with a dash of Chardonnay and Malvasia Bianca, it literally bespeaks of "terroir." Very sophisticated!

Photo by Anna Pakula

ORVIETO DOC (UMBRIA)

Well-known DOC area that is located in the southwestern part of Italy's Umbria region and that produces about two-thirds of Umbria's DOC wines. It covers a large area surrounding the hilltop town of Orvieto, with a Classico zone covering a smaller area at the center. Wines from this Classico area are generally better. Orvieto produces mostly dry, ordinary white wines from Trebbiano, Malvasia Verdello, Grechetto, and Drupeggio grapes. The sweeter wines of this DOC (Abboccato, Amabile, or Dolce) are better, especially those made from grapes infected with Botrytis Cinerea, which engenders a rich, honeyed flavor. It's thought that Orvieto's abboccato-style wines were favored in the middle Ages; they were also prized by Pope Gregory XVI in the nineteenth century.

Marcello's recommendation:
Orvieto Bigi, Orvieto La Carraia

FRASCATI DOC (LATIUM)

DOC zone located in the Castelli Romani area on the southeast edge of Rome in Italy's Latium region. It encircles the town of Frascati and neighboring environs. Frascati produces more wine than any other DOC in Latium, most of it dry white wine (made from Malvasia, Trebbiano and Greco) that is a favorite in Rome restaurants for House wine, Frascati wines can also be Amabile, Dolce, or cannellino, the latter a special version using very ripe grapes hopefully infected with Botrytis Cinerea . A Spumante version is also produced.

Photo by Anna Pakula

Marcello's recommendation:
Fontana Candida Frascati
Principe Pallavicini Frascati

TREBBIANO D'ABRUZZO (ABRUZZO)

White wine grape that is grown in southeast Italy, primarily in Apulia and Abruzzi, but also in Marche and Latium. Bombino Bianco generally produces bland, low-alcohol wines used primarily with other grape varieties for blends, and sometimes for Vermouth. In Abruzzo, a DOC called Trebbiano D'Abruzzo uses this grape, which is also called Trebbiano D'Abruzzo (although it is unrelated to Trebbiano). Some producers in this DOC carefully prune the Bombino Bianco vines, thereby reducing the yield and generating more flavorful grapes, which result in wines that can be quite good. The better examples exhibit creamy and citrusy characteristics. Bombino Bianco is also known as Zapponara Bianca.

Marcello's recommendation:
Valentini Trebbiano D'Abruzzo
Masciarelli Trebbiano D'Abruzzo
Zaccagnini Trebbiano D'Abruzzo
Illuminati Trebbiano D'Abruzzo

Photo by Anna Pakula

Photo by Anna Pakula

Photo by Anna Pakula

Fiano Di Avellino (Campania)

One of Southern Italy's most famous white wines. It is produced in the Campania region, from vines grown on the volcanic hillsides of Avellino, east of Naples. Richly flavored, medium-bodied white. Light, straw-yellow color with appealing aromas and flavors of ripe pears, honey and toasted hazelnuts. At its best after a year or two in the bottle, Fiano will age up to five. Fiano's racy acidity makes it perfect for foods with high fat content: triple creme cheeses, salami, sausages, etc. Can also be used to add acidity to a wine-friendly salad dressing.

Marcello's recommendation:
Terre Dora Fiano D'avellino
100% Fiano D'Avellino Grape. Clear gold. Quite aromatic, almonds and beeswax and fresh white fruit. Ripe and fresh, flavors follow the nose, mouth-filling and long, a really excellent wine. Fermented and aged entirely in stainless steel, it's all fruit, seeing no oak at all.

Others:
Mastroberardino Fiano di Avellino
Feudi San Grecorio Fiano di Avellino
Di Maio Norante Fiano di Avellino
San Paolo Fiano di Avellino

Greco di Tufo (Campania)

The earliest written record of Greco di Tufo dates back to the most famous Latin writers: Varrone, Virgilio and Columella (in its treaty on agriculture, De re rustica) when the vine was known as 'Aminea Gemina Minor', from the shape of its bifid cluster. The most ancient of the native Campanian vine, from which the famous homonymous white is made, Greco di Tufo DOC has gained in the course of time a world reputation together with the Taurasi D.O.C.G. The grapes mature in October, fear frost and express better characteristics in a narrow area of the Irpinia, where they meet the ideal pedo-climatic conditions. The cluster is medium-small, the berry spherical, of yellow colour, dotted with rose.

Marcello's recommendation:
Greco Di Tufo Mastroberardino
100% Greco Di Tufo Grape. Clear pale gold. Lovely scents of honey and hazelnuts lead into a full-bodied flavor, crisp and tart apples and pears, with hazelnut nuances that mirror the nose. Clean fruit and zingy acid linger in a long finish. A very fine wine.

Others:
Greco Di Tufo, Feudi Di San Grecorio

Photo by Anna Pakula

FALANGHINA (CAMPANIA)

The Sannio Falanghina vines are planted at up to 1600 feet above sea level in the breath-taking area of Benevento and the surrounding provinces. Selected clay and calcareous soils, along with a southwestern exposure, make this area ideal for the aromatic perfumes and intense flavors of Falanghina. The wine goes through partial malolactic fermentation at controlled temperatures in stainless steel to preserve its unique flavors of peach and banana. This wine shows a straw yellow color with greenish nuances. The nose denotes good personality with intense, clean and elegant aromas of acacia. In the mouth it is crisp yet balanced, with pleasant yet intense flavors and a persistent finish.

Photo by Anna Pakula

Marcello's recommendation:
Sannio Falanghina Vesevo
100% Falanghina From Campania.
Pale gold with elegant, intense aromas of apple, banana and pineapple. Medium-bodied with a lingering aftertaste of citrus and minerals. Delicious with seafood, mozzarella and pasta with tomato sauce.

Others:
Falerno del Massico Villa Matilde,
100% Falanghina
Sannio Falanghina Villa Matilde,
100% Falanghina
Fontanavecchia Falanghina Del Taburno, *100% Falanghina*

INZOLIA (SICILY)

The white wine Inzolia has similar characteristics than other whites from Southern Italy and France. It is a complex wine that's rich, full-bodied and with a lovely deep golden colour. The flavor is bolstered with exotic fruit and the finish is generally dry and slightly bitter. Due to the fullness, it is definitely a food wine and is delicious with appetizers, seafood and pasta.

Marcello's recommendation:
Solia antichi vinai, *100 % Inzolia from Sicily.* This Sicilian native is an increasingly valued component of dry white wines, offering softness and smoothness.

From Around the Globe

CABERNET SAUVIGNON (ITALY, FRANCE, CALIFORNIA)

Cabernet Sauvignon is certainly the most successful and popular of the top-quality red wine grapes. It is the primary grape of most of the top vineyards in Bordeaux's Medoc and Graves districts in France. It's also the basis for most of California's superb red wines. This reputation for excellence has launched a Cabernet Sauvignon popularity boom around the world. Cabernet Sauvignon has begun making inroads into areas of Spain and Italy where local grapes have dominated for centuries. The flavor, Structure, Complexity, and longevity of wines made from the Cabernet Sauvignon grape are what make it so popular. Its fruity flavors have been described as cherry, black cherry, black currant (cassis), and raspberry. In addition, other flavor descriptors include Minty, The Acids and Tannis found in a Cabernet Sauvignon wine help form the basis for its structure and longevity. In Bordeaux, Cabernet Sauvignon is most often blended with one or more of the following: Merlot, Cabernet Franc, Petit Verdot, or Malbec. In California, wines are more often made with 100 % Cabernet Sauvignon grapes.

The Cabernet Sauvignon grape has been grown in Italy for over 150 years, it has only recently become more popular. Italian winemakers are now blending small amounts of Cabernet Sauvignon with the local top red wine grape, Sangiovese. They also make a few top-quality wines with a majority of Cabernet Sauvignon. There are a multitude of well-made Cabernet Sauvignon-based wines made throughout the world. Among the most notable wines are those from France's Château Lafitte-Rothschild, Château Latour, Château Mouton-Rothschild, and Château Margaux and California's Beaulieu Vineyards, Caymus, Mondavi, Jordan and many more.

Marcello's recommendation:
Caymus, Napa, CA, **Estancia,** CA, **Charles Krug,** Napa CA, **Turnbull,** Napa, CA, **Chimney Rock,** Napa, CA, **Jordan Sonoma, Opus One Mondavi-Rothschild,** Napa, CA,
Far Niente, Napa, CA,
Turnbull, Napa, CA
Freemark Abbey Bosche, Napa, CA
Pedroncelli Dry Creek, CA
Raymond Estate Reserve, Napa, CA
Robert Mondavi, Napa, CA
Mondavi "Reserve," Napa, CA
Stags Leap "Reserve," Napa, CA
Rutherford Hill, Napa, CA
Solaris Cabernet, Napa, CA
Honig Cabernet, Napa, CA
Robert Mondavi Vineyards, Napa, CA
Freemark Abbey Sycamore, Napa, CA
Columbia Crest, Columbia Valley, WA
Mezza Corona, Trentino, Italy

MERLOT (ITALY, FRANCE, CALIFORNIA)

Though commonly referred to as simply Merlot, this red-wine grape is really Merlot Noir (there's also a Merlot blanc variety). Merlot is the primary grape in Saint-Émilion and Pomerol, and one of two primaries (the other being Cabernet Sauvignon) of Bordeaux. Merlot acreage in the Département of Gironde, which encompasses most of Bordeaux, is almost twice that of Cabernet Sauvignon. However, Merlot has never been as highly regarded as Cabernet Sauvignon, which dominates in the Médoc and Graves-growing areas that produce wines traditionally viewed as Bordeaux's most important. Much of the wine world views Merlot as simply a grape to be blended with Cabernet Sauvignon or Cabernet Franc. Still, Merlot can produce great wines like those of Pomerol's Château Pétrus, which makes one of the world's most expensive red wines, most of which are 100 percent Merlot. Merlot is also widely planted in other areas of France. Growers in the Languedoc-Roussillon region, for instance, are being encouraged to plant this grape in order to improve the vast quantities of wine produced there. Merlot is extensively grown throughout the world but has developed a tarnished reputation from overproduction in areas like northeastern Italy. It's an extremely important grape in Italy's Fruili-Venezia Giulia and Veneto regions. In California and Washington, Merlot was initially planted as a blending grape, but in the late 1970s it began to stand on its own as a variety and has been continually gaining popularity. California Merlot acreage has continued to increase, as have the number of wineries producing Merlot wines. California's, generally regarded as a leading producer of quality Merlot wines, has been producing them since the late 1970s. In French the word Merlot means "young blackbird," probably alluding to the grape's beautiful dark-blue color. Compared to Cabernet Sauvignon, Merlot grapes ripen fairly early and have lower Tannins and higher sugar levels. They produce wines that are generally softer and with slightly higher alcohol content. High-quality Merlot wines are medium to dark red in color, rich, and fruity, with characteristics of black currant, cherry, and mint. Merlot wines are rounder and more harmonious than Cabernet Sauvignons and usually can be enjoyed much earlier. Generally, Merlot wines do not age as long as Cabernet Sauvignons. A small amount of Cabernet Sauvignon or Cabernet Franc is often blended with Merlot grapes to give the wine a bit more structure.

Photo by Anna Pakula

Photo by Anna Pakula

Photo by Anna Pakula

Marcello's recommendation:
Merlot Boscaini
100% Merlot.
In Veneto, this varietal has found a particularly favorable environment Ruby color with red and violet reflections. Beguiling aroma, discreetly fruited with the slightest accents of herbs. This wine is smooth and rounded with the soft tannins consistent with a premium Merlot. A perfect companion to grilled meats and saffron risotto and others most full-flavored dishes. Serve at room temperature.

Others:

Sterling Merlot, Napa, CA
Delicato Merlot, CA
Beringer, "Napa Valley" CA
Mietz Cellar Merlot, Sonoma, CA
Merlot Zamo & Zamo (Friuli)
Mezza Corona, Merlot, Trentino, Italy

Ferrari Carrano Merlot, Sonoma, CA
Hogue Cellars "Genesis," Napa, CA
Mionetto Merlot Piave, Trentino, Italy
Ferrari-Carano Merlot, Sonoma, CA
Clos du Bois Merlot, Sonoma County, CA

CABERNET FRANC
(FRANCE, ITALY, CALIFORNIA)

The somewhat leaner sister of cabernet sauvignon, cabernet franc is often grown in the same places and is usually blended with cabernet sauvignon and merlot. The one noteworthy exception to this is the Loire Valley of France where cabernet franc alone makes the well-known wines Chinon and Bourgueuil. Cabernet franc often has a unique violet aroma and a slightly spicy flavor.

Marcello's recommendation:
Masùt Da Rive Cabernet Franc, Italy

Photo by Anna Pakula

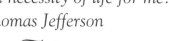

Good wine is a necessity of life for me.
—Thomas Jefferson

Brotherhood Winery photo archives.

Pinot Noir (Italy, France, California, New York State)

The red grape of France's Burgundy region. Pinot Noir is been grown in France for over 2,000 years. The Pinot wine is described as "genetically unstable," meaning that it mutates very easily, which makes consistency from this vine extremely difficult. There are estimates of over 1,000 different types or clones belonging to the Pinot family. Some, such as Pinot Blanc, Pinot Gris or Grigio, and have become well-known varieties on their own. The combination of Pinot Noir's mutating characteristic and difficult growing requirements (a long, cool growing season) makes this variety a frustrating grape from which to make wine This situation is aggravating for Pinot Noir lovers as well, because the gap between the high and low quality of this wine is broader than any of the other important reds. The flavor of Pinot Noir is chameleon like. When young, good wines exhibit the simpler fruity characteristics of cherries, plums, raspberries, and strawberries. As these wines mature, they display a variety of Complex characteristics including chocolate, game, figs, prunes, Smokiness, truffles, and violets. Pinot Noir is also an important red grape In northern Italy, Pinot Noir is known as Pinot Nero There are some very good Pinot Nero wines that come out of Italy's mountainous areas. There's been a great deal of effort in the United States to emulate the great Burgundy Pinots. Some of California's better Pinot Noir wines come from the state's cooler regions such as Carneros the Russian River Valley, and parts of Santa Barbara counties. Oregon's long, cool growing season is conducive to the production of some delightful Pinot Noir wines.

Marcello's recommendation:
Torti (Oltrepò Pavese Pino Nero) (Italy)
Made from 100% hand-harvested Pinot Nero, the grapes are cold fermented and the wine is aged 18 months in barrique to bring out this noble, full-bodied cardinal red wine with orange reflections. It is beautifully balanced, rich and elegant with a bouquet of blackberry and raspberry jam and subtle toasty flavors. A perfect complement to red meats, fowl, pasta dishes with hearty sauces and strong cheeses.
Pinot Noir Brotherhood (NY State)
Silky smooth with well defined fruit redolent of red berries with cherry notes.
Medium-bodied with soft tannins, concluding in a pleasing finish.

Brotherhood Winery photo archives.

Others:
Camelot, Santa Barbara CA
Kendall Jackson "Vintner's Reserve" CA
W.H. Smith "Hallenthal Vineyard," Sonoma, CA
Cambria "Julia's Vineyard," Santa Maria California
Mazzolino Oltrepo Pavese DOC 100% Pino Noir, Italy

Camelot, CA
Calera Central Coast, CA
9th Island, Tasmania Australia
Handley, Anderson Valley CA
Chalone Estate, CA
Trinchero, CA

ZINFANDEL - PRIMITIVO (ITALY, FRANCE, CALIFORNIA)

Grape that is considered California's red-wine grape because it's not widely grown in other parts of the world. Rapidly gaining acceptance by California growers, and it is now that state's most extensively planted red grape. For years Zinfandel's origins were very mysterious. Now, however, a relationship between Zinfandel and Primitivo (a variety grown in Italy's Puglia region) has been established. Outside of the Zinfandel grown in California (and Italy's Primitivo), there are only isolated plantings of this grape- mainly in South Africa and Australia. Zinfandel is vinified in many styles, which vary greatly in quality. One popular style is White Zinfandel, a fruity-flavored white wine that's usually slightly sweet and ranges in color from light to dark pink.

Photo by Anna Pakula

Zinfandel styles to hearty, robust reds with berrylike, spicy (sometimes Peppery) flavors, plenty of tannins and alcohol, and enough depth, complexity, and longevity to be compared to Cabernet Sauvignon. Occasionally, Zinfandel is fortified and marketed as a California Port-style wine. The Italian DOC, Primitivo Di Manduria, produces dry red Primitivo grape-based wines that are similar to some California Zinfandel. As Zinfandel's popularity increases, more and more enterprising Italian Primitivo growers are labeling their wines "Zinfandel" and exporting them to the United States.

Marcello's recommendation:
Primitivo Zinfandel Le Corte
100% Primitivo that was harvested in early September from head pruned vines. The wine was aged in 1-2 year old, predominantly American barrique for 12 months prior to bottling. A ripe, rugged, medium-to-rich Primitivo with aromas and flavors that are reminiscent of plum and berry jam.

Photo by Anna Pakula

Ravenswood Dickerson Zinfandel
From California this wine is an exciting, lively wine redolent of all the intense fruit character that this Napa Valley location is capable of. It is bursting with the essence of blackberry, violets, licorice and eucalyptus. It is dense and sweet in the mouth, with strong flavors of ripe berries, chocolate, coffee and spicy oak. Finishes with full, ripe tannins and the flavor of mint.

Others:
Ermaedes Mendocino, California
Seghesio, Sonoma California
Storybook Mountain, Napa
Rosenblum Zinfandel, CA
Ravenswood Zinfandel, Mendocino CA
Beringer White Zinfandel, CA
Montevina, White Zinfandel, N. Coast
Ca'ntele Primitivo del Salento, Italy
Pervini Primitivo di Manduria Archidamo, Italy

SHIRAZ & SYRAH
(ITALY, FRANCE, CALIFORNIA, AUSTRALIA)

Known as Syrah in France & Shiraz in Australia in the USA, it can appear under either name depending on the style of the winery. The grape is though to be named for a city in Persia (Shiraz) where it probably originated. It produces full rich wines of intense color and flavor. In warmer climates like Australia, the grape produces wines that are sweeter and riper tasting. In cooler climates like the Rhone Valley of France, it often has more pepper and spice aromas and flavors.

Marcello's recommendation:
Lindemans Shiraz, South Australia
Sobon Estate Syrah, Shenandoah Valley
Stonehaven Shiraz, Limestone Coast Australia
Saint Hallet Shiraz, Barossa Valley Australia
Penny's Hill Shiraz, Mc Laren Vale Australia
Stags Leap Petite Syrah, Napa California
Annata"Nadarìa" Syrah, Sicily Italy
Spadafora "Sole dei Padre" Syrah, Sicily Italy

Photo by Anna Pakula

Photo by Anna Pakula

Other varietals grapes from the world

Sparkling and White

CHAMPAGNE (FRANCE)

Even though effervescent wines abound throughout the world, true champagne comes only from France's northernmost wine-growing area, the Champagne region, just 90 miles northeast of Paris. This renowned region consists of four main growing areas-Montagne de Reims, Côtes de Blancs, Vallée de la Marne, and the Aube. Because it's so far north, Champagne's cool weather creates a difficult growing environment for grapes. The main grape varieties-red Pinot Noir and Meunier and white Chardonnay-all require warmer weather for optimum development. Grapes that don't fully ripen tend to have high acidity and less-developed flavors, which just happen to be the perfect formula for Sparkling wine Dom Pérignon, the seventeenth-century cellar master of the Abbey of Hautvillers, didn't invent sparkling wines, he is acknowledged for greatly improving the process. He's credited for his work in preventing champagne bottles and corks from exploding by using thicker bottles and tying the corks down with string. Even then, it's said that the venerable monk lost half his champagne through bursting bottles. Dom Pérignon is also celebrated for developing the art of blending wines to create champagnes with superior flavor. Today, some champagne makers mix as many as 30 to 40 or more different base wines to create the blend, or Cuvée. Most major champagne houses strive for a cuvée that's consistent from year to year. Good champagne is expensive not only because it's made with premium grapes, but also because it's made by the Méthode Champenoise. This traditional technique requires a second fermentation in the bottle, as well as some100 hand operations (some of which are mechanized today).

Photos by Anna Pakula

In Vino veritas
Nel vino la verita.
English translation: In wine the truth.

Marcello's recommendation:

Nicolas Feuillatte
  Brut "1ere Cru"
Montaudon Brut Mousseux
Laurent Perrier Brut
Laurent Perrier
  "Cuvée Rosé" Brut
Moët & Chandon
  "Dom Pérignon"
Krug "Grande Cuvée"
Comtes de Bucques Brut
Taitinger "La Française"
Billicart Salmon Brut
Ruinart Champagne Reims
Veuve Clicquot Champagne
Deutz Champagne

Photo by Anna Pakula

Photo by Anna Pakula

Champagne verses sparkling wine

Only sparkling wine made in the Champagne region of France can be called Champagne, even if it is made from the same type of grape as Champagne using the same production techniques. Sparkling wine in Spain is referred to as cava, in Germany it is called sekt, and in Italy it is called "spumante". Sparkling wines made in the U.S. by the same method of production used in the Champagne district in France are sometimes labeled as "Méthode Champenoise" wines.

Italy

Marcello's recommendation:
Ferrari Brut
Maurizio Zanella Franciacorta Brut Ca Del Bosco
Berlucchi Brut

United States

Piper Sonoma, Blanc de Noir
Domain Chandon
Gloria Ferrer, NV Brut

Photo by Anna Pakula

Photo by Anna Pakula

Photo by Anna Pakula

CHARDONNAY (ITALY, FRANCE, CALIFORNIA, AUSTRALIA)

Chardonnay has taken the lead for first-class white-wine grapes. Chardonnay is being extensively planted throughout the world. Chardonnay is easy to grow and quite versatile. Their flavors can be described as Buttery, Creamy, Nutty, and Smoky, popular fruit descriptors include Apple lemon, melon, and pineapple.

Chardonnay's origins are difficult to determine but-as with many popular wines-its reputation was established in France, particularly in the Burgundy region. Chardonnay is also an important grape in the Champagne district where it's picked before fully ripe while it still has high Acid and understated fruit flavors-the perfect combination for champagne. California has adopted this grape with fervor and has come into prominence with its delightful Chardonnay wines from wineries such as acacia, Kittler, Robert Mondavi, Jordan, Shaffer, Farniente. In addition to the hundreds of wineries in California, there are some 200 wineries producing Chardonnay wines in other parts of the United States. Chardonnay has also seen a tremendous planting surge in Australia, with excellent wines from several wineries including Petaluma. As this grape's popularity grows, new vineyards of Chardonnay are being planted throughout the world in Italy, New Zealand, South Africa.

Photo by Anna Pakula

Photo by Anna Pakula

Robert Mondavi

Marcello's recommendation:

Ferrari Carano Reserve (Napa, California)

90% Napa, 10% Sonoma

A wine in an elegant, well-balanced style, not full of butter an oak like some Reserve Chardonnays. From our cool, windy vineyards in the Carneros region of Napa County come grapes with clean bright acidity and intense aroma. From Our Alexander Valley vineyards in Sonoma County come the rich, tropical notes of classic California Chardonnay. The two sources combine to yield a wine that is beautifully focused and balanced between fruit and oak, with elegance and finesse.

Robert Mondavi (Napa, California)

A stylish and graceful wine, Robert Mondavi Napa Valley Chardonnay has beautifully integrated apple, citrus and white flower character. Complex notes of mineral and oak spice weave through the smooth, silky fruit flavors and linger on the finish.

Cervaro Antinori Castello della Sala (Umbria)

80% Chardonnay, 20% Grechetto Taste: Very fruity and complex on the nose, with hints of vanilla and excellent varietal character. In the mouth it is structured with a very long finish.

Coppo Chardonnay "Coste Bianche" (Piedmont)

Made from 100% Chardonnay grown in varied vineyards around Canelli and Agliano. Fermentation is started

Photo by Anna Pakula

in stainless steel tanks and completed in 1-2 year old barrique where it is aged for 5 months, although a portion does remain in tank and is only blended into the final wine. Malolactic fermentation is partially carried out.

Costebianche reveals Pale yellow hues with golden reflections and a bouquet of lemon accented by light vanilla and spice. The wine is soft and subtly buttery on palate with toasty oak nuances and a long, pleasant finish.

Sonoma Cutrer Russian River Valley (Sonoma, California)

White Wine Chardonnay from Sonoma-Cutrer Californian. At first the scent is creamy, yet clean, with essence of delicate green pear. With time in the glass, the flinty wet stone aroma takes over, coupled with overtones of rich, yeasty Champagne.

Photo by Anna Pakula

Others:
Beringer, Napa, CA
La Pietra Cabreo, Tuscany Italy
Shafer, Napa CA
Planeta Chardonnay, Sicily Italy
Far Niente, Napa, CA
Raymond Chardonnay, Napa, CA
Silverado, Napa Valley, CA
Saint Clement Carneros, Napa, CA
Kendall Jackson, California
**Jermann Dreams Venezia,
   Giulia, Italy**
Jordan, Sonoma CA
**Mezza Corona Chardonnay,
   Trentino, Italy**

SAUVIGNON BLANC (ITALY, FRANCE, CALIFORNIA)

White grape of the famous Sancerre region in France, as well as New Zealand. Sauvignon Blanc also grows in Bordeaux (where it is usually blended with Semillon), South Africa, and in California and Washington state. Its wonderfully wild, untamed flavors are often reminiscent of grass, herbs, green tea and limes, often overlaid with a smokiness. In California, sauvignon Blanc can also take on green fig and white melon flavors.

Marcello's recommendation:
Camelot Sauvignon Blanc (California)
Flavors of soft fig and herbs coupled with
a crisp citrus finish make this Sauvignon Blanc a terrific aperitif or the perfect companion to shellfish, spicy Asian
cuisine or salads.
Sterling Sauvignon Blanc (Napa)
Clear medium straw in color. Sauvignon Blanc offers aromas of ripe fresh tropical fruit - pineapple, mango and passion fruit with hints of crisp lemon and fresh apricot. On the palate the wine shows notes of ripe fresh pineapple and mango, refreshing Meyer lemon, with a dry, clean finish.

Others:
Beaulieu Vineyards, Napa, California
Sancerre Belles Vignes, Loire, France
Mason, Napa California
De Sante, Napa, California

Photo by Anna Pakula

RIESLING & GEWÜRZTRAMINER (ITALY, FRANCE, CALIFORNIA, GERMANY, SOUTH AFRICA)

Riesling is considered to be one of the world's great white-wine grapes and produces some of the very best white wines. It's a native of Germany, where it's believed to have been cultivated for at least 500-and possibly as long as 2,000-years. The Riesling grape's ability to retain its acidity while achieving high sugar levels is what creates wines with considerable aging potential. Riesling wines are Delicate but Complex and are characterized by a Spice, Fruity flavor (that's sometimes reminiscent of peaches and apricots); Riesling is vinified in a variety of styles ranging from Dry to very sweet. There are extensive Riesling plantings in California where early wines were made in a Dry, oakey style. California winemakers now produce high quality, German-style Rieslings, which are lighter, more delicate, and slightly to medium sweet. Other states that have had success with Riesling wines include Oregon, Washington, and New York. Australia has extensive plantings of this grape and produces high-quality Riesling wines, particularly from the Eden and Clare Valleys. France's Alsace region and Italy's Alto Adige also produce excellent Rieslings.

Marcello's recommendation:
Brotherhood Reisling, New York State
Semi-dry white wine with fruity aroma. Perfect with spicey food this Riesling is one of the best growing in the New York state.

Others:
Cave Spring Riesling, Canada
Hogue Riesling, Columbia Valley, California
Handley Gewürztraminer, Anderson Valley, California

Photo by Anna Pakula

Seyval (France, USA)

One of our most popular white wine grapes is the Seyval Blanc. This French-American Hybrid was released in 1919 by Bertille Seyval and Victor Villard. This cultivator is considered by many to be one of the finest of the French-Americans. It ripens mid-season to large, compact, conical bunches of slightly elliptical greenish-yellow berries. A well-made Seyval blend can compete favorably with Chardonnay, or Pinot Blanc. Seyval Blanc has become the premier French-American white wine grape in the east as well as in England.

Marcello's recommendation:
Brotherhood Seyval Blanc.
From NY state oldest winery our Seyval Blanc is a crisp, attractively fruity and moderately dry table wine. We very carefully handpick only the best bunches, gently crush and press them, and then put the juice through a slow, cool fermentation.

Other wines most made by blending two or more grapes varietal

Duca di Salaparuta Colomba Platino (Sicily)
Straw yellow-colored wine with greenish effects through-out. The bouquet is intense and the taste is pleasantly fruity and harmonic. Made of Inzolia and Grecanico grapes.

Regaleali Bianco Tasca d'Almerita (Sicily)
Made from Inzolia, Sauvignon -Tasca, Catarratto Straw yellow in color with a delicate and persistent bouquet of apples and ripe fruit. Dry and pleasant with excellent structure and aromatic persistence. Recommended as an aperitif or with all types of fish and seafood dishes.

Maculan Pino & Toi (Veneto)
60% Tocai, 25% Pinot Bianco, 15 % Pinot Grigio.
A remarkably light-bodied, refreshing, crisp white... possesses loads of fruit and a refreshing, perfumed style.

Others:
Silvio Jermann Vintage Tunina (Friuli)
  Complex blend of Chardonnay, Sauvignon, Malvasia, Ribolla & Picoliti. Aged without oak, with aromas of anise, citrus fruit, pear, honey and spring flowers.

Venica & Venica Tre-Vignis (Friuli)
  Tocai, Chardonnay & Sauvignon grapes
Santa Margherita Luna dei Feldi (Trentino)
A blend of Chardonnay, Traminer and Müller-Thürgau, this single-vineyard wine has a full, intense, fruity aroma.

Donnafugata Chiarandà (Sicily)
50% Ansonica, 50% Chardonnay
This is a wine with personality and elegance. Aromas of ripe yellow fruit, apples and notes of peaches and vanilla fused with peanut butter. Round flavor and mouth-filling.

Zaccagnini Il Bianco di Ciccio (Abruzzo) A white varietal from
southern Italy, blend of Greco & Trebbiano grapes.

Mastroberardino Lacrima Christi Del Vesuvio Bianco (Campania)
The Napolitans' wine of kings. Crafted exclusively from the historic Coda de Volpe varietal (to mean tail of the fox - a name given by Pliny the Elder after the shape of the grape clusters), Mastroberardino's 1998 Lacryma Christi del Vesuvio Bianco is fruit-filled, spicy, offering great depth. We found it medium-bodied with a nose hinting flavors of liquid minerals, honey, and piecrust. It's been likened to an exquisite dry Riesling with the taste of Mediterranean sun at its soul. You'll note it to be extremely well made, exhibiting intrigue as well as charm from its delicate, pale yellow robe all the way through to its lingering, classy finish.

Donnafugata Anthìlia (Sicily)
50% Ansonica, 50% Cattaratto
This wine shows a precise personality linked with extremely sweet and elegant fruit sensation and notes of yellow peach and plums.

Photo by Anna Pakula

Red Blend

Marcello's recommendation:
Illuminati Lumen (Super Abruzzan)
This wine is primarily Montepulciano blended with a varying percentage of Cabernet Sauvignon, depending of the outcome of the harvest. This is an elegant, dry red wine, very rare & collectable.

Terre D'Agala Grape Narello Mascarese and Merlot (Sicily)
With mild winters and dry summers, the Duca di Salaparuta wines are exposed to ideal growing conditions on the hillsides of Sicily. Terre D'Agala is considered the offspring of Sicilian tradition, with an international taste. An intense, ruby red wine with violet effects present in the glass, Terre D'Agala possesses a fragrant bouquet with a rich variety of sensations and well-blended fruit and oak flavors. Terre D'Agala has a refined and elegant taste that blends consistently with the body and bouquet.

Photo by Anna Pakula

Photo by Anna Pakula

Ramitello di Maio Norante (Molise)
Made from 80% Montepulciano, 20% Aglianico.
The Montepulciano was harvested in October while the late-ripening Aglianico wasn't picked until November. The wine was aged in large oak barrels for 2-3 years. Ramitello undergoes a light filtration prior to bottling. The wine displays an intense ruby red color with violet reflections. The scent of plums comes through on the nose while on the palate, the wine is full bodied and velvety with a perfect balance between the flavors of plum and wood berries. Hints of licorice are evident in the persistent finish.

Colli Picchioni Rosso (Latium)
A blend of Merlot, Sangiovese, Montepulciano and Cabernet Sauvignon harvested in early October and vinified entirely in stainless steel tanks. Blended in equal parts, this wine is super fresh on the nose. The fresh fruit carries through to the palate which also exhibits a touch of salt and tobacco.

Lacrima Christi Rosso Mastroberardino (Campania)
80% Piedirosso 20% Aglianico. Lacryma Christi is one of the oldest wines hailing from Campania, and also one of the most legendary. According to legend, when Lucifer was cast from Heaven, he managed to take a strip of Paradise for his own.

As Lucifer descended from Heaven, the strip of Paradise fell from his grasp, and it landed in the Gulf of Naples. Seeing what Lucifer had done, the Lord wept and His tears fell on the land between Vesuvius and Sorrento, thus giving life to the vines. Lacryma Christi literally translates from Italian as "Tears of Christ."

Others:
Monacesca Camerte (Marche)
This new "Super Marche" is a blend of Sangiovese grosso (70%) and Merlot (30%), which was first produced in 1997 to wide-spread international acclaim. The sangiovese and merlot are vinified separately and aged for six months in new French oak. The final assemblage is undertaken and the blend is aged in Allier barriques for a further six months. The wine combines the elegance and smoothness of sangiovese with the power of merlot cultivated in the Matelica area. The fusion of character and elegance, combined with sweet tannins imparted by contact with new oak, produce a wine that is not only drinkable upon release but which will benefit considerbly from ageing for up to ten years.

Hofstätter Rosso "Yngram" Vino da Tavola (Alto Adige), *70% Cabernet Sauvignon, 25% Petit Verdot, 5% Syrah.*

Gnemiz Ronco del Gnemiz (Friuli)
40% Merlot 60% Cabernet Deep ruby red color. Aromas of red berries & earth. Soft tannins, full bodied &structured. An impressive mouthful of wine now with a spectacular potential for aging.

Donnafugata Tancredi (Sicily)
70% Nero D'Avola 30% Cabernet. The two varieties fuse in fine style. The Cabernet gives the Nero d'Avola a touch of mint, enriching its substantial supply of scents. The flavors are well structured, full, absorbing and remarkably persistent.

Montevetrano (Campania)
60% Cabernet Sauvignon, 30% Merlot & 10% Aglianico. Grown in the estate vineyards at Montevetrano. The wine was fermented in stainless steel tanks & aged in new barriques from the Département of Allier in France, Nevers and Tronçais (name of towns in France) for 12 months. The wine is unfiltered and exhibits deep ruby red hues in the glass. The nose is intense with a bouquet of red berries, tobacco and leather. On the palate the wine is dry and full-bodied with firm tannins. Montevetrano is very distinctive in character with a rich structure and elegant flavors.

Photo by Anna Pakula

Colle Picchioni Vigna del Vassallo (Latium)
60% Merlot, 35% Cabernet Sauvignon, 5% Cabernet Franc
Vigna del Vasallo is brilliant ruby red in color with a full bouquet of violets, iris, pine, wild fruit & toasted oak. It is dry, round, full-bodied & rich through a lingering finish.

Apicella Costa d'Amalfi Tramonti Rosso (Campania)
Wine made from Tintore & Per'e Palummo grapes is grown on the slopes of the Amalfi coast. Scented with pleasant notes of tobacco and soft fruits.

Chimney Rock "Elevage" (Napa California)
51% Merlot, 42% Cabernet Sauvignon, 7% Petit Verdot

Ferrari Carrano Sienna (Sonoma California)
Made of Sangiovese, Cabernet Sauvignon & Malbec grapes.

Estancia Meritage (California)
Cabernet and other bordeaux blend.

Quintessa (California)
Quintessa is the Quintessential wine estate. Quintessa the wine is a blend of the best vineyard lots of Cabernet Sauvignon, Merlot and Cabernet Franc all grown on the estate's 170 acres of vineyards in the heart of Rutherford. The winery's stone facade is combined with natural landscaping of native plants and oak trees to create a subtle presence amidst the diverse terrain. The natural design facilitates a gentle, gravity flow system from the moment the grapes arrive at the winery. Once the wine is in barrel, it will age in caves that have been dug into the hillside behind the winery.

Dessert Wines

These are sweet wines that are served with (or instead of) dessert. Examples include like port and sherry, and late harvest wines, which are made from grapes that have shriveled a bit, concentrating their sweetness. As a rule of thumb, a dessert wine should always be sweeter than the dessert.

Others:
Colosi Malvasia Delle Lipari (Sicily)
Ben Rye Passito di Pantelleria Donna Fugata (Sicily)
Batasiolo Moscato d'Asti "Bosc dla Rey" (Piemonte)
Deinhard Beeren, Auslese (Germany)
Castellare Vino Santo - San Niccolo (Tuscany)
Banfi "Florus" Late Harvest (Tuscany)
Moscadello di Montalcino (Tuscany)
Chiarlo Moscato d'Asti - Nivole (Piemonte)
A delicate sparkling wine made from the Moscato grape.Beautiful straw color and gentle sweet flavor with hints of almond are the dominant characteristics of this famous wine.
Duck Walk Gewürztraminer "Late Harvest"
   (Long Island, NY)
Hunt County Ice Wine (Finger Lakes, NY)

Photo by Anna Pakula

Photo by Anna Pakula

SHORT DESCRIPTION OF ITALIAN WINES

Asti Spumante: sparkling sweet or semi-sweet white wine often drunk for celebrations. Produced in the Asti district of Piedmont.

Barbaresco: dry, full-bodied red wine from Piedmont

Barbera: dry, spicy red wine from Piedmont

Bardolino: light, dry red or rosé wine from the Veneto

Barolo: good, full-bodied red wine from Piedmont

Brunello di Montalcino: superior, powerful red wine from Tuscany

Chianti: light, rosé-style wine from the Tuscany

Cinqueterre: dry, light and fragrant white wines from Liguria

Est! Est! Est!: crisp, fruity white wine from region near Rome

Frascati: crisp, fresh, dry to off-dry white wine from near Rome

Lacrima Christi: full-bodied wine from Campania and Sicily

Lambrusco: slightly sparkling wines from Emilia-Romagna

Marsala: dark dessert wine from Sicily

Merlot: good, dry red wine from NE Italy

Montepulciano: dry red wine from Abruzzi

Moscato: sweet, aromatic white wine from NW Italy

Nebbiolo: light, red wine from Piedmont

Orvieto: crisp, smooth, dry white wine from Umbria

Pinot Bianco: dry white wine from NE Italy

Soave: dry white wine from the Veneto

Valpolicella: light, fruity red wine from the Veneto

Verdicchio: fresh, dry white wine from the Marche

Verduzzo: dry, tangy white wine from NE Italy

Vernaccia di San Gimignano: dry white wine from Tuscany

Vin Santo: golden, scented wine ranging from sweet to dry, Tuscany

SPIRITS & LIQUEURS

Amaretto: sweet almond-flavored liqueur

Cynar: strongly flavored artichoke-based digéstif

Digestivo: slightly bitter, herb-flavored liqueur to help digestion

Grappa: strong spirit from grape pressings, often laced in coffee

Sambuca: aniseed liqueur, served with 3 coffee beans (*that means Love, Health and Happiness*)

Strega: strong herb-flavored liqueur

Vecchia Romagna: Italian brandy

Marcello on a small vineyard in his hometown of Riccia.

Marcello Russodivito archive

(below left) Marcello's friend, Romeo Caraccio in his wine cellar in Rome at Agata e Romeo Ristorante;
(below, right) Quattro Passi Ristorante's wine cellar in Nerano, Sorrento, Italy

Archive of Agata e Romeo Ristorante

Quattro Passi Ristorante archive

Photo by Anna Pakula

Phot by Anna Pakula

(above) Photos by Anna Pakula

Marcello Russodivito

Biography

On the beautiful Southeastern shore of Italy touching the sparkling blue waters of the Adriatic Sea is the Molise region. Established in 1963, this mostly mountainous area has an economy highly dependent on agriculture and the raising of livestock. This land can trace its history back to the last days of the Roman Empire. Surviving mass invasions from then up to the newly-created Kingdom of Italy in 1861, the Molise region continued to suffer severe economic conditions and mass emigration of its inhabitants to more industrial areas of Italy. After 1861, the borders of the region were fixed along the Fortore and Volturno rivers, and in 1964 the Molise region became independent from Abruzzi. In 1970, 52 municipalities were separated out to form the Province of Isernia. Campobasso itself

Marcello's family in Italy
(left to right) brothers, Antonio and Adolfo, Marcello, his mother, Vittoria, brother, Lino and sister, Giusy

has been the capital of the Molise region since 1806, and was once known as an internationally famous area for cutlery craftsmanship. Comprised of many small villages, Campobasso's old town was abandoned in the 18th century, and a new town

Fireworks at the tower in Marcello's hometown of Riccia

was established on a fertile plain below the magnificent Montforte Castle with its six towers dating from the 13th century. Visitors today can marvel at the beautiful pastoral setting, good food—the Molise baby lamb is particularly famous—and the awe-inspiring churches reminding the villagers of their rich heritage. One such village of 7000 inhabitants, Riccia, is the ancestral home of Marcello Russodivito. It is roughly 70 miles from Naples and a three hour drive South of Rome. In this small picturesque

Left to right: Lucio, Nicola, Tullio and Marcello

village, Marcello began his career. Born one of five children, his father a tailor and taxi-cab driver and his mother a housewife, Marcello can trace his roots and interest in the culinary profession back to his earliest childhood.

It was a long-standing tradition for Italian families to have their children become apprentices in various businesses. Therefore, it was not unusual for Marcello, at age 7, to frequent coffee houses and restaurants in the village square, delivering espresso, soda, and cappuccino requested by local businesses. In exchange for this service, the young Marcello would not accept any money, however, he did not refuse the offer of an occasional ice-cream. His father supported his commitment and even bought him a waiter's jacket for his Communion when he was 9 years old instead of a more traditional gift. His father recognized Marcello's interest in the hospitality industry, but he never saw the realization of Marcello's talents since he passed away one week after the Communion Service. Marcello was motivated to work hard and plan for a culinary profession. This was helped by a close connection to a bar/restaurant owned by a friend of the family. His guiding philosophy at this time was inspired by his brother, Lino, who told him that in order to be successful one must become

Marcello entered the cooking school at 14 years old.

Marcello winning a trophy during a soccer game.

familiar with all aspects of one's intended profession. The analogy he used was very appropriate. In building a house, one must build a strong foundation first, but be aware of other parts of the building as well. In a culinary profession, one must be thoroughly familiar with the front of a house—the dining room—as well as the back of a house—the kitchen. With this in mind, Marcello enrolled at age 14 in the Culinary High School of Montecatini Terme after he completed junior high school.

Because of cultural shock in a completely new and intimidating environment, Marcello wanted to quit; indeed, having once been looked up to as a leader by other children in the village, he was overcome by the strangeness of his new situation, and his growing loneliness away from his familiar surroundings.

Fortunately, he had the support of his family and he decided to immerse himself in the new culture and dialect of the area. In six months he felt more comfortable and was able to integrate himself into his

studies. He separated himself from his former life in Riccia for two years, only taking vacation breaks to visit his two brothers in Rome. In this way, Marcello became familiar with two important areas of his preparation for culinary success: how to interact with the public in the front of the restaurant and, in addition, learning the complex operations which make up a successful kitchen operation in the back of the restaurant.

Marcello began his apprenticeship confidently; his drive towards success in a culinary career grew stronger. Like a sponge, he wanted to absorb every facet of the business. He wanted to understand the roles played by chefs, waiters, and owners of restaurants. Traveling extensively in Europe over the course of a year, he was learning languages and picking up cooking tips in various seasons. This meant that he learned a variety of techniques at least four times a year in different localities. Styles in food preparation varied by region, and he sought experiences with wide-ranging types

Marcello serving his army tour of duty

of food, and skills in their presentation. The mastery of his craft grew over a five-year period; he had little time for relaxation or vacations. This exposure to the foods of Germany, France, England, and Switzerland would come in handy in later years.

One of his personal desires at this time was to work in a warm climate, but this would have to be postponed as he prepared for his mandatory army registration, which he began at age 19. While in the army, Marcello was stationed in Rome, where he had a fortunate opportunity to be near his mother, and also find some work in local restaurants to enhance his culinary training.

After his army tour of duty had ended, Marcello went to England where he learned the English language. He still wanted to enjoy a warmer, less humid environment, however, even to the extent of considering a move to Hawaii. When an opportunity presented itself to work in Bermuda as a breakfast chef, Marcello jumped at the chance. In Bermuda, as his mastery of cooking increased, he was offered a better position in an Italian restaurant, and it was at that time that he experienced one of the happiest moments of his life: he met a vacationing American lady who was to become his future wife. He even considered a job in New York in a Hilton Hotel so that he could be near her. In fact, he commuted from Bermuda for three months. When he decided to remain in Bermuda, his romance developed quickly, and his fiancé came to Bermuda to seek employment. Both Marcello and Carolyn decided to go back to Italy after a year where Marcello again moved around several regions gaining valuable experience. It wasn't long before Marcello and Carolyn were married.

Marcello working into the front of the house in Rome.

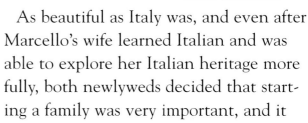
Marcello working with friend Rocco while in Bermuda

As beautiful as Italy was, and even after Marcello's wife learned Italian and was able to explore her Italian heritage more fully, both newlyweds decided that starting a family was very important, and it would be best to return to New York. In 1983, they moved to Rockland County, New York. While there, Marcello decided to work in the dining room of a restaurant rather than the kitchen, where the quality and preparation of the food left something to be desired. His high expectations and standards for the highest quality of food and service led Marcello to several other restaurants in search of that special quality he had come to expect for his customers. He would not accept compromises on the quality of food offered to the public.

Marcello and his wife, Carolyn

In frustration, Marcello began looking for locations where he could rent and open his own restaurant. Other restaurant owners recognized Marcello's talents, even offering him multi-year contracts to secure his services. But Marcello had developed a mastery of his craft that he wanted to share with others, both in food preparation and in teaching other young hopefuls in the profession. While he was not considering a partner at this time, Marcello checked other locations in Westchester County,

Marcello and his daughters Nicole and Danielle

New York. He and his wife were living in his wife's grandparent's basement apartment. This was planned to be a stay of three months; however, three months became ultimately three years. During the first three months, Marcello was actually fired from a restaurant because it became known that he was actively seeking his own place. He wanted to return to Italy, but he bided his time and took a temporary job in a New Jersey restaurant. The owner of this restaurant had a major influence on Marcello's thinking. The owner had told him that he would not accomplish his goals by burying himself in a village in Italy. Rather, he should follow his dream of independence, and use his extraordinary talents in New York. Even though he was offered a position as a Maitre'D in the restaurant, Marcello was encouraged to seek fulfillment of his dream to have his own restaurant. Many years ago, as a 14-year old, Marcello always had his sights on this goal.

As an immigrant in America, Marcello realized that he had to face many challenges before he could achieve his goals. He recognized the importance of maintaining his determination to succeed; he was basically a fighter for his ideals. Nothing would prevent him from focusing his passion on qualities of loyalty and devotion to customers and staff which form the basis for a successful culinary endeavor.

After two months in Rockland County, Marcello's frustration increased. His intolerance for shoddy working conditions and general inefficiency and incompetence in the restaurant where he was employed was extremely discouraging. He felt that merely pushing for high volume at the expense of quality was not fair to the public, who certainly deserved more value for their money. He felt that everything occurring both in the dining room as well as the kitchen should enhance the dining pleasure for the customers. Anything less would be a betrayal of professional standards. As Marcello's frustration grew, he realized increasingly that he must do more to find a location in

Before it was Marcello's Ristorante it was a bookstore.

The 10th Anniversary of **Marcello's of Suffern**

which he could further his dreams. Interestingly, a fortuitous stroke of fate would provide Marcello with the means to start on the path to his goal.

One day, while looking over various rental possibilities, he was searching for a house in Garnerville. On his way, he took a wrong turn and found himself on Lafayette Avenue in the Village of Suffern. He noticed a building with a For Rent sign, and in this building, which had formerly been a bookstore, he saw a real estate broker, who by chance happened to be on the premises. Marcello learned that the rent was very affordable, and the building could be easily renovated for the creation of a restaurant. He saw at once that it was here that his dream could be realized; and so was born Ristorante Marcello of Suffern.

Marcello did not want to spread himself too thinly and get a partner—his father-in-law used to say that "partners were only good for dancing." However, after ten years in Suffern, Marcello noticed that a coffee shop across the street was in bad shape, and was drawing the wrong kind of clientele. He saw an opportunity to open an outdoor café. He bought the shop and gave one of his waiters, Mark McGuy an opportunity to become his partner. The result was a successful opening of Café Dolce. The menu was greatly extended to provide a great variety of foods, and it became a full-fledged restaurant. Marcello could now turn some of his responsibilities over to his partner. Café Dolce became a wonderful addition to downtown Suffern.

After successfully owning two restaurants for 3 years, Marcello had a chance to open an upscale restaurant in New Jersey, Once again, he broke his no-partnering rule and joined with another man to open a bistro in Saddle River, New Jersey. There were good prospects for success, but nothing panned out due to septic tank problems at this site.

Shortly thereafter, however, Marcello learned of the availability of the fine, up-scale Ho-Ho-Kus Inn in Ho-Ho-Kus, New Jersey. The potential was overwhelming, and renovations soon began on this magnificent building which had even served as a temporary headquarters for George Washington in the Revolutionary Period in the 18th century. Marcello dedicated a great deal of time to this new venture, while the Suffern restaurant was languishing. With his characteristic zeal, Marcello upgraded his original restaurant energetically. He added a new bar and developed new catering possibilities. Once again, business was booming in his Suffern restaurant. He bought out his partner in the Ho-Ho-Kus Inn and sold Café Dolce to Mark McGuy. Once more, he was a solo owner.

*The grand opening for the **Ho-Ho-Kus Inn***

Group of Marcello's relatives during a cooking demonstration in the new cooking studio.

Cooking class 15 years ago in Marcello's main kitchen.

He traveled frequently between the restaurants in Suffern and Ho-Ho-Kus to oversee the maintenance of quality food and service about which he had always been very strict.

With the success of both restaurants, Marcello had time to visit his family and friends in Italy, participate in their wine festivals, and devote time to his passion for great food and its preparation. He joined other famous chefs in publishing tested recipes, shared his expertise in many cooking demonstrations requested by various corporations, and started an ongoing series of cooking classes at the Suffern restaurant.

Marcello's first cookbook, Signature Pasta *published by La Cucina Italiana Magazine (including 5 of his recipes) in collaboration with 24 other chefs.*

Marcello interacting with Mr. and Mrs. D'Antonio.

Dom DeLuise visits **Marcello's of Suffern** *with Bruce Nubile, Michael Vingiello, Aniello Vacchiano and Marcello.*

View of landscape in Tuscany.

He decided to produce his own cookbook featuring some of his favorite recipes based on his many years of experience. In this way he would continue to share the great traditions of Italian cooking which have been part of his heritage from those early days in the Molise region of Italy, and in some of the finest restaurants in Europe and America. The end result, offered for your dining pleasure, is the book now in your hands.

Buon Appetito!

Marcello teaching his daughters' class how to make ravioli.

Marcello's Ristorante of Suffern

Marcello's Ristorante of Suffern opened its doors in 1986.
If you read the biography, it will tell you a little bit more about how
Marcello ended up in Suffern. *Marcello's Ristorante of Suffern* is
an accomplishment and, below, you'll see how Marcello's looked in
the beginning and, to the right, how it looks today.

Marcello's Ristorante of Suffern
21 Lafayette Avenue, Suffern, NY 10901 • (845) 357-9108
For all major information about Marcello's services,
visit our website www.marcellosgroup.com

HO-HO-KUS INN HISTORY

The Ho-Ho-Kus Inn is Jersey sandstone structure believed to date from the 1790's. The stories about its origin are so many and so contradictory that it is difficult to find the actual facts.

Originally it was the private residence for the John "Jake" Zabriskie family in the era immediately following the Revolutionary War. He prospered with his mills and owned most of the business section of Ho-Ho-Kus and the northern Turnpike which amounted to 57 acres plus 50 acres in what is now known as Ridgewood.

When Zabriskie died, the building continued as a private home for a time it even served as a parsonage for the Christ Episcopal Church in Ridgewood. The Ho-Ho-Kus Inn had many names: The Zabriskie House, The Villa Inn, The Mansion House The Wayside Inn and The Washington Inn.

Wealthy people from New York, who spent their summers in Newport and Tuxedo Park, would stop at The old Mansion House while the owners and horses rested and refreshed themselves before the long journey ahead.

The old Mansion House was about to be torn down in the late 1920's when Mrs. H.T.B

Jacquelin purchased it thus saving for future generations that reminder of past times. It became an Inn and a long line of Managers and owners were involved.

In 1941, the town bought the Inn and in 1943 leased it to Mr. Edward Brindle. Mr. Brindle painted the entire interior dark green-including the Kitchen!

Helen Wilson and her brother Gordon Butler leased the Inn in 1953 and opened the Tap Room in 1957. Followed by the Inn proper in 1958. The Inn was restore to the full beauty it knew the post-Revolutionary War era.

In 1998 Marcello Russodivito decided to purchase the History of the Inn by opening his second Italian restaurant after Ristorante of Suffern, NY.

What does the Indian name Ho-Ho-Kus mean? There are so many interpretations, but the most accepted is that Ho-Ho-Kus was a contraction of Mehohokus, a Delaware Indian term meaning "The red Cedar". Who can dispute that Ho-Ho-Kus is an easy name to remember. And equally memorable we hope will be each of your visits to the Inn which proudly bears the Ho-Ho-Kus name.

In 2000, Marcello invited famous restaurateurs Romeo Caraccio and Agata Parisella from the famous restaurant in Rome, *One Michelin Star Agata & Romeo* Via Carlo Alberto 45, Rome, Italy, http://www.AgataeRomeo.it/ to do the reinauguration of the Ho-Ho-Kus Inn changing from continental cuisine to Italian creativity cuisine with a touch of continental with a four-day event of menu tasting from Rome.

Marcello's Ho-Ho-Kus Inn

One East Franklin Turnpike, Ho-Ho-Kus, New Jersey 07423 • (201) 445-4115
A historical landmark since 1870.
For all major information about Marcello's services visit our website www.marcellosgroup.com

M̲ost of the recipes that you will find in this cook book are all tested with the scanpan cookware. I am proud to promote SCANPAN cookware from Denmark. I think it is fantastic cookware and every home should have at least 1 or 2 pieces, if not a whole set. We've been using SCANPAN in our commercial kitchens and my cooking studio and it has made a great impact in our cooking because it cooks fast as well as evenly. The pans are non-stick and dishwasher safe and that has made my dishwashers very happy. Visit my gourmet store on my website www.marcellosgroup.com for more information about this fantastic cookware or if you would like to make a purchase.

Marcello testing food with ScanPan.

SCANPAN Ceramic Titanium CLASSIC NEW TEK Cookware is manufactured in Denmark by SCANPAN Denmark AS. SCANPAN Denmark, today the largest European manufacturer of pressure cast aluminum cookware, was founded in 1956. Modern, functional Scandinavian design combines with old world craftsmanship to present SCANPAN Ceramic Titanium CLASSIC NEW TEK Cookware. SCANPAN CLASSIC NEW TEK has been available in the US since January 2002 and succeeds the original SCANPAN Titanium. SCANPAN CLASSIC NEW TEK features an updated, patented surface technology that is still using our patented ceramic-titanium foundation as its base but works with a new non-stick compound with a different chemical and molecular structure. The result is a "closed" non-stick surface that is now offering perfect food release all the time and no longer requires pre-oiling or seasoning before use and is dishwasher safe.

The surface of SCANPAN CLASSIC NEW TEK is based on a number of different patents. The original surface was first introduced in Europe in 1986 and in the US in 1987. SCANPAN 2001+ Cookware, as it was

then called, caused an immediate stir in the cookware market since it was the first cookware, and is still the only cookware, that combines a professional cooking utensil with long-term non-stick convenience, backed by a genuine full lifetime warranty. Each time that consumer publications have tested cookware between 1987 and 2000, SCANPAN Cookware was consistently awarded "Best Non-stick Cookware" ratings and "Best Buy" recommendations.

The best way to understand SCANPAN's technology is to take a step back and look at traditional non-sticks. They are great in releasing food. That's about where most of them stop. And we all know how annoying it is to keep the breakfast sausage, bacon and eggs in that tiny circle in the middle of the pan to cook and fry — move them to the side, and the sizzle stops. Somehow the handles always seem to be just about falling off. And the pans themselves sometimes have warped and curled into undulating metal that won't sit still on that burner, losing contact with the heating element. Over time, the non-stick surface comes off, finds its way into the food, and it is time to buy a new non-stick pan. Again. Then there are the more expensive, more heavy-duty pots and

pans. They cook evenly, have no hot spots, and you can use metal utensils. But, the food sticks to these "traditional pros" unless we use a lot of butter or other seasoning. That's where SCANPAN CLASSIC NEW TEK comes to the rescue. We start with the best tradition in professional cookware: Pressure-cast aluminum. Aluminum is an excellent conductor of heat. The SCANPAN heavy-duty base is literally forged into shape under 200 tons of pressure. That's the only way to really eliminate hot spots and to create a perfectly even pan base. And we have researched the optimum thickness for the pan base to prevent any warping and, at the same time, create the perfect condition for the pan to heat up quickly and evenly. Our combination of raw material, pressure casting and thickness of the pan body, thus, results in perfectly even heat distribution, superior heat retention and a perfectly flat pan base for life.

SCANPAN Cookware is especially engineered for halogen, ceramic and electric ranges but will, of course, work on gas and electric coil ranges, as well. Now to SCANPAN's space-age surface: Both ceramic and titanium are incredibly hard materials. After having pressure-cast the raw pan body, the ceramic-titanium compound is super-heated to 36,000° F (thirty six thousand degrees!) at which point it liquifies. The ceramic-titanium enters a "plasma state". That liquid plasma is then fired into the pan surface at twice the speed of sound. Lots of heat and impact. The ceramic-titanium literally anchors itself in the aluminum surface and becomes one with the pan. That's NASA technology. The SCANPAN surface technology is based on the principle of using ceramic tiles on the space shuttle, which prevent the shuttle from burning up during re-entry into the earth's atmosphere. We have that concept patented for aluminum non-stick cookware.

When looking at SCANPAN CLASSIC NEW TEK under a microscope, we see something like a lunar landscape. A myriad of mini-craters, all similar in size and shape. These craters were created when firing the ceramic-titanium compound into the cooking surface, and are then filled with our specially formulated NEW TEK non-stick compound. The compound is in the craters, not on them. The ceramic-titanium protects it from being scraped away. Even if you use a metal spatula. We have tried. Ran a metal spatula with a 2-lb-weight over the SCANPAN surface 300,000 times. A third of the spatula was literally ground away

after the test (performed by an independent laboratory in Germany). The pan's non-stick surface and performance remained perfectly intact!

The MOHS scale measures hardness of gemstones. Diamonds come in with a perfect 10. SCANPAN CLASSIC is a 9.5. There is no tool in your kitchen that could damage or destroy the SCANPAN surface. If we can't destroy the surface, we can't get at the non-stick compound. If we can't get at the non-stick compound,

it can't be scraped away. If we can't scrape it away, it will work for as long as you own the pan. It's in there for keeps! *This is truly the last non-stick pan you will ever have to buy (pardon our using this rather overused phrase!).* And we guarantee it with a full lifetime warranty.

There are a few other things that set SCANPAN CLASSIC NEW TEK apart from the rest of the field: Tired of lifting hot metal lids to see what's going on with your food? Our glass lids solve the problem and let you see what's cooking. They are interchangeable, too, between pots and pans and sauté pans. And yes, they are available separately. Tired of loose or wiggly handles that seem to barely hang on by the threads of their screws or rivets? Our patented spring-lock handles won't come loose. No room for food particles to hide behind the rivets and create a haven for bacteria. And they stay cool on the stove, no need for cumbersome handle sleeves. And the whole line is oven-safe to 500° F. Great for finishing off puffy omelets, or preparing that roast or casserole. Or even baking cookies and corn-bread in a SCANPAN fry pan! SCANPAN CLASSIC NEW TEK is unique in its technical construction and non-stick surface. And it is the easiest to use and to clean: The new SCANPAN CLASSIC NEW TEK surface requires no pre-oiling or seasoning. Heat the pan to working temperature and start preparing your meal. After use, clean the pan in the dishwasher, or by hand with warm, soapy water and a brush.

"These are excellent non-stick pans. These pans are perfect for cooking fish, crab cakes and other foods that tend to "break up" when turning them. Even risotto. As a chef I have used many fry pans in my career. Never one like this! Everything about these pans far exceeded my expectations. I recommend this pan for the novice and pro alike!"

For nearly 50 years, SCANPAN Denmark has been at the *forefront of inventing* advanced cookware technology to make life easier both for the hobby chef and the serious cook. Today, we offer a wide variety of cooking tools that combine *solid craftsmanship* and *construction, latest surface technologies* and *attractive designs* all covered by the SCANPAN LIFETIME WARRANTY.

Uova all'Occhio di Bue con Spinaci, Prosciutto, Pomodoro e Mozzarella

Over Easy Eggs with Spinach, Italian Ham, Tomatoes and Mozzarella   Serves 1

oven roasted tomatoes
  (see page 21)
2 oz. spinach
1 slice prosciutto
1 slice mozzarella
salt and pepper to taste
2 tbsp. olive oil

1 Preheat oven at 400°. In a ScanPan, 8" or 9" heat 1 tbsp. olive oil and sauté spinach for 30 seconds until wilted. Set aside.

2 Clean pan with paper towel, put pan back into the fire. Break 2 eggs into a bowl. Heat olive oil for a few seconds and drop the eggs into the pan. At the same time put one slice of mozzarella, spinach, tomatoes and prosciutto into a corner of the ScanPan. Bake for 1 minute. To serve, slide eggs into a plate and serve right away.

Asparagi Gratinati al Parmigiano

Gratin of Asparagus with Parmigiano   Serves 2

See recipe page 82

Marcello on duty with his chefs and manager.

As you can see in most of the food photography of this cookbook, I utilize the beautiful ceramics of Ceramiche D'Arte of Ravello Italy's Amalfi Coast. All artwork from the Ceramiche D'Arte line are decorated using colors and patterns which were once used in ancient times. Ceramics have been useful to man for many centuries. They are used to hold food as well as a means of artistic expression thanks to the use of glazing and pictorial decorations. Visit my Gourmet Store on my website www.marcellosgroup.com for more information or to make a purchase.

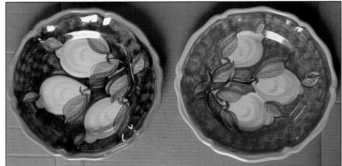

al dente To cook pasta until it is tender, but still firm to the bite.

arborio rice Italian short grain rice most commonly used in Risotto (see below).

bouquet garni Combination of herbs and spices: bay leaves, thyme, black pepper corn and parsley.

capellini Literally, the name of this pasta means "fine hair". Capellini are only slightly thicker than "capelli d'angelo" (angel hair pasta).

cavatelli Short oval pasta with ridges, native of Apulia and common in other Southern Italian regions.

ciufoli Hand-made pasta cut similar to "cavatelli."

deglaze To dissolve the remaining bits of sauteed or roasted food in a pan or pot by adding a liquid and heating.

ditalini A short tubular pasta best used in soups, in pasta e fagioli and similar rustic preparations.

egg wash Egg yolk or white mixed with a small amount of water or milk.

gnocchi Better known in their fresh form (most often made with potatoes and four), gnocchi are also sold dried. They are hollow in their dried form, and most closely resemble conchiglie or shell-shaped pasta, but are slightly more open and have scalloped edges. Some are ridged, others are not.

linguine Native of Liguria, this pasta (literally "little tongues") is thin, fat and long.

mascarpone cheese A thick Italian cream cheese.

orecchiette Shaped like little ears, hence their name; a classic in Apulia and other Southern Italian regions.

pancetta Italian style, unsmoked bacon cured with salt & pepper.

panco Japanese bread crumbs that can be found in the Oriental section of food markets.

penne One of the most widely used short pastas, shaped like old pens. Penne are not ridged unless the package specifies other wise; their diagonally cut ends are excellent for picking up sauces, both dense and light.

polenta Specially ground cornmeal cooked in either stock or water, which may be enriched with butter, cream, cheese or eggs. When cooled, its consistency is firm enough to be sliced and grilled.

prosciutto Italian-style raw ham, a specialty of Parma, cured by dry-salting for one month, then air-drying in cool, curing sheds for another 11-17 months. Usually cut into tissue-thin slices, the to better appreciate its intense flavor and deep pink color.

radicchio A leafy endive with reddish-purple leaves and creamy white ribs and a mildly bitter flavor.

ramekin A small dish used for baking or serving.

rigatoni Wide, tubular pasta about 2" long, with straight-cut rather than diagonally cut ends, always ridged.

risotto A classic Northern Italian dish that is made from certain varieties of medium-grain rice that have an outer layer of soft starch. During cooking, the rice is stirred constantly while hot liquid is gradually added, causing the starch to dissolve and form a creamy sauce that complements the chewy rice. Arborio is by far the best known and most widely available in the United States.

san marzano A plum tomato growing in San Marzano village in the Campania region of Italy, easy to find in good supermarkets.

spaghetti Among the most famous of pasta shapes, spaghetti owe their name to the word spago, meaning "string", because that is what they most closely resemble. Cylindrical and long, they are sometimes called vermicelli (meaning "little worms") in Campania, although vermicelli are slightly thicker.

speck Speck is a pork product made from a boned ham that is moderately salted and seasoned, cold-smoked and then well aged.

temper To bring to a desired consistency, texture or hardness by blending, mixing or kneading.

trenette Slightly wider than linguine, this pasta is thin, flat and long.

zest The thin, outermost layer of a citrus fruit peel which contains most of its aromatic essential oils.

Index

Vegetables

Side Dishes

Sauce

Dessert

The bell tower in Riccia. (left)
One of the streets of the old section of Riccia. (right)

Marcello's hometown Vicoli of Riccia.

Winter in Riccia.

Winter in Riccia.

A view of Riccia with a tower.

Riccia